JUSTIN WILSON'S
Outdoor Cooking With Inside Help

JUSTIN WILSON'S
Outdoor Cooking With Inside Help

Photographs by
JEANNINE MEEDS WILSON

Pelican Publishing Company
GRETNA 1986

First printing, September 1986

Library of Congress Cataloging-in-Publication Data

Wilson, Justin.
    Justin Wilson's outdoor cooking—with inside help.

    Includes index.
    1. Barbecue cookery.   2. Cookery (Smoked foods)
3. Cookery, American—Louisiana style.   I. Title.
II. Title: Outdoor cooking-with inside help.
TX840.B3W55   1986   641.5'784   86-16867
ISBN 0-88289-609-1

Photograph on page 50 courtesy
Al Godoy, Louisiana Tourist Development Commission.

Manufactured in the United States of America
Published by Pelican Publishing Company, Inc.
1101 Monroe Street, Gretna, Louisiana 70053

*This book is dedicated to the peoples
of Louisiana, who put the fun in pleasure,
even when they are cooking wondermous food
for their friends and families.*

CONTENTS

Foreword by Gus Weill 9

Introduction by Jeannine Meeds Wilson 11

How to Make a Roux 15

Appetizers 17

Salads 29

Sauces 43

Soups and Gumbos 53

Breads 61

Seafood 69

    How to Peel a Crawfish 71

    How to Crack a Crab 75

Meats 93

Game 109

La Boucherie 117

Vegetables 127

Desserts 145

Index 157

FOREWORD

With no trouble at all you can imagine him on the veranda of some old southern mansion, julep in hand, wide brimmed plantation hat tilted just so. Obviously, this gentleman is a southern colonel . . . or a southern corporal . . . or a southern something.

The suit is white or cream colored, the string tie hangs casually, like it's waiting for a dare.

You're in the old South.

And then he talks. And the old South never sounded like that. The accent is Cajun . . . or maybe it's not! He has this habit of switching back and forth. It's musical, but what planet he happens to be representing at the moment strongly affects his speech. There is always laughter in it, school-boy laughter amused at . . . well, maybe *you!*

His eyes dance. Sometimes they jitterbug and you have to wonder what is this courtly gentleman doing jitterbugging in his head!

Written all over him is a zest for life. He loves it! If he ever has a bad day just he knows it, and you have the feeling that he chases those rare moments away with the cane he carries jauntily.

And then he cooks. And you're almost certain that you've stumbled upon some festival being put on by angels. Nobody cooks like Justin Wilson because Justin Wilson is cooking to his own music.

This amazing man has managed to capture the indescribable magic of great Cajun cooking. He's been cooking all his life and to Justin Wilson it's a wild adventure all the way.

His ingredients are unique, and what he does to them . . . what he mixes in . . . a toss of this, a pinch of that . . . a change . . . a taste . . . a smacking of lips . . . the result is beyond mere language.

You've got to taste it. And then you've got to let your friends taste it.

The man and his recipes are one and the same.

Both are quite wonderful.

So come meet Justin Wilson. Draw up a log, sit on the ground, let the old master do his tricks.

You'll be entertained and your palate will take time out from tasting to help the rest of your mouth shout, "Gimme some more!"

GUS WEILL
Spring, 1986

9

These beautimous peppers are the base of the seasoning in South Louisiana.

INTRODUCTION

From the time that the first Acadians set foot on the Gulf Coast in the last part of the 18th century, they have spent most of their time outside. It's true that many of them preferred the solitude and inaccessibility of the swamp, fearing that they might be rounded up and displaced again, but another reason was that they were not welcome in New Orleans and the other towns. The Creoles' rigid class system didn't have a place for these penniless, disinherited fishers and farmers, so they continued up the Mississippi River into the bayous to places like St. Gabriel, St. James, and French Settlement. Soon afterward they moved westward onto the prairie.

In such small settlements, isolated from cities and strangers, the Cajuns thrived. They took what the land and waters offered them and forged a culture that endures today. They had no sources for expensive spices, so they used what they gathered and grew in their gardens: cayenne pepper, onions, garlic, and parsley. Louisiana has huge deposits of salt, which they took advantage of, and the Indians showed them the secrets of many native plants like sassafras. Cajun cooking is full of crawfish, turtle, alligator, and all kinds of fish and wild game because these animals are plentiful and easy to catch.

Today in Louisiana Cajuns preserve their culture through daily practice. Families and friends gather in their yards to cook while they relate their experiences. Everyone cooks, and everyone has a story to tell. They don't hurry. As a result, there is no such thing as Cajun fast food.

Cajuns cook outdoors because they are practical. Louisiana's climate makes outdoor living possible twelve months of the year. Beautiful trees and flowers, dark streams, and sluggish bayous provide moving pictures that no television could match. Besides, many of the foods prepared by Cajuns don't fit in a kitchen. Can you imagine 50 pounds of crawfish in a kitchen sink, or a 70-pound pig on a counter? There is always plenty to eat at a Cajun house. The rest of the family or more friends may drop by.

Cajuns are practical people, but they will try anything. Justin Wilson says that Cajun cooking is imagination and common sense in the proper proportions. As their ancestors did, they take what the land and waters give them and make something wonderful.

Some of the results of this attitude—imagination tempered with common sense—appear on these pages. Follow Justin's suggestions and experiment with these recipes, keeping in mind that cooking is a pleasure. Do it as the Cajuns do: outside and with your friends. You'll have your enjoys, I garontee.

JEANNINE MEEDS WILSON

JUSTIN WILSON'S
Outdoor Cooking With Inside Help

14

HOW TO MAKE A ROUX

———————◆———————

Plain flour
Oil—bacon drippings, olive oil, lard, cooking oil, or a
mixture of these.

When I want to make a t'ick roux I use 3 parts flour to 1 part oil. To make a t'in roux use 2 parts flour to 1 part oil.

Put oil into a heavy pot. A black iron skillet or Magnalite pot works well. Pour in the plain flour and stir to mix well. Cook on medium or low heat and stir as the roux begins to change color. You can see that I usually cook my roux until it gets to be a very dark brown. My roux sometimes takes more than an hour to cook. Some peoples get unpatient wid' that, but I use that time to think about many things. When I cook a roux I relax myself. And you should also, too. Be careful not to let your roux burn. You got to stir a roux damn near all the time while it cook itself. Me, I got a special spoon that I use only to stir my roux. It has worn itself plum flat to the shape of the skillet.

After my roux is cooked all the way plum' it gets a shine on it. Now add chopped onions, celery, and bell pepper. Be careful not to add too much celery and bell pepper; they are taste killers. When the onions are clear add chopped parsley, green onions, and garlic. After these cook a little bit I pour in some cold water and stir. The roux will separate, then come back together. Now you can add the other things to make a gumbo, sauce piquant, or gravy.

Some people make a roux in a microwave oven. They say it's much faster than this method. Well it is, but why cook if you can't have your enjoys. This recipe that I'm just tole you has worked for me for more than 60 years and it's worked for many other peoples in South Louisiana. Also, too, it taste more better.

Appetizers

Devilish Eggs
Crab Meat Alma
Pickled Shrimp #1
Pickled Shrimp #2
Andouille in Comforting Barbecue Sauce
Smoked Pickled Eggs
Chicken Gizzards and Oysters in Wine
Italian Sausage in Tomato Sauce
Oysters Ed
Crabby Mushrooms
Tasso
Tasso Pizza on French Bread
Boiled Peanuts

These blue crabs are pretty, yeah, but I like dem much more better after they are cook. Or in a salad or cocktail.

DEVILISH EGGS

6 hard-boiled eggs, peeled
2 TBS. mayonnaise
2 TBS. poupon mustard
1 TBS. Louisiana hot sauce

1 TBS. pimentos, mashed
3 TBS. dill relish
Salt, to taste

Cut the eggs in half. Remove yolk from white and set white aside. Mash yolks with a fork and add the mayonnaise and the rest of the ingredients. Spoon mixture back into egg whites and serve on a bed of lettuce.

CRAB MEAT ALMA

1 stick butter or margarine
1 small bunch green onions,
   chopped
½ cup finely chopped parsley
½ cup finely chopped celery
1 small can mushrooms, drained
3 TBS. flour

2 cups light cream
2 cups grated Swiss cheese
½ cup sherry or dry Vermouth
Ground cayenne pepper
Salt, to taste
1 lb. white crab meat or cooked
   shrimp

Melt butter in heavy saucepot. Sauté vegetables until soft. Blend in flour and add cream. Heat until thickened. Add cheese and heat until it has melted. Add wine, cayenne pepper, and salt. Fold in crab meat or shrimp. Heat gently for 8 to 10 minutes.
Serve with french bread or in patty shells.

Alma is a good cook and also a fine, good friend, who has a terrific sense of humor, I garontee!

PICKLED SHRIMP #1

1 cup olive oil
1½ cups white vinegar
¾ cup lime juice
2 tsp. Louisiana hot sauce
½ cup honey
4 TBS. capers

2 tsp. salt
½ tsp. celery seed
2 lbs. raw small or medium
  shrimp, peeled
2 medium white or purple
  onions, thinly sliced

Mix all of the liquid ingredients in a large bowl. Stir in the honey until it is dissolved. Add capers, salt, and celery seed and stir well. This sounds like it will be raw, but the lime juice will cook the shrimp. Add shrimp and onions. Stir. Let set overnight.

PICKLED SHRIMP #2

2 qts. water with 2 tsp. salt
2 lbs. small or medium shrimp,
  peeled
2 tsp. salt
¾ cup lime juice
2 tsp. Louisiana hot sauce
1 cup olive oil

1½ cups white vinegar
½ cup honey
½ tsp. celery seed
4 TBS. capers
2 medium white or purple
  onions, thinly sliced

Put shrimp in boiling salted water. Cook for 1 minute, and cool quickly. Mix all of the liquid ingredients and salt in a large bowl. Stir in the honey until it is dissolved. Add celery seed and capers and stir. Then add shrimp and onions, stirring some more. You can eat this after it marinates for about one hour, but it won't hurt to let it set overnight.

Some people use sugar, but I use honey because I like it. This will make enough pickled shrimp for a small party. Be sure to use teeth-picks, not your fingers.

ANDOUILLE IN
COMFORTING BARBECUE SAUCE
———————◆———————

4 cups finely chopped onions
1 cup finely chopped celery
1 cup finely chopped bell pepper
1 cup finely chopped fresh parsley
1 cup peanut oil
2 TBS. finely chopped garlic
3 cups steak sauce

½ cup Louisiana hot sauce or 2
  tsp. cayenne pepper
3 cups ketchup
3 tsp. salt or to taste
1 cup Southern Comfort liquor
1 lb. andouille sausage

Sauté onions, celery, bell pepper, and parsley in peanut oil until the onions are clear or tender. Add garlic and cook a little longer. Add steak sauce, hot sauce, and ketchup. Add salt to taste. Add Southern Comfort. Bring to a boil. Lower heat and cook for 2 to 3 hours.

Makes about ¾ gallon. This will keep in the refrigerator for weeks.

Slice 1 lb. andouille or smoked sausage ¼ inch thick and combine with 1 cup sauce. Heat well on stove or in a chafing dish. Serve with small pieces of french bread or use teethpicks to spear andouille. You will need plenty of napkins, also, too.

Other smoked sausages may be used, but we like andouille.

SMOKED PICKLED EGGS
———————◆———————

1 dozen eggs
Vinegar—4 parts vinegar, 1 part
  water
5 or 4 tsp. smoked salt, to taste
Hot pepper (fresh from the
  garden or pickled)

1 small bay leaf or ½ tsp. dried
  mint
4 or 5 large cloves of garlic, cut in
  large pieces

Hard-boil eggs by bringing to a rolling boil. Cut down to a boil that does not bubble and cook for 20 minutes. Cut fire off and let eggs sit in hot water for 30 minutes. Run cold water over eggs to cool. Peel eggs and put in a jar that can be either sealed or closed tightly. Put in bay leaf, pepper, garlic, and smoked salt. Cover eggs well with vinegar and water mixture. Put the lid on the jar.

Let them sit 2 to 3 weeks in the vinegar, then eat.

All these hoovey-doovies look so good I believe I'll jus' push up a chair and make a meal from dem.

CHICKEN GIZZARDS
AND OYSTERS IN WINE

2 TBS. olive oil
1 lb. gizzards
1 TBS. Lea & Perrins
   Worcestershire sauce

2 tsp. Louisiana hot sauce
1½ cups dry white wine
1 tsp. salt
1 pint oysters

Put olive oil in a large skillet. Add cleaned gizzards, Lea & Perrins, Louisiana hot sauce, wine, and salt. Bring to a boil. Cover. Cut fire down and cook slowly until gizzards are getting tender. Keeping fire low, add oysters. Do not boil mixture. Oysters are done when their edges curl.

Serve hot in a chafing dish.

Serves 12 people.

ITALIAN SAUSAGE
IN TOMATO SAUCE

2 lbs. Italian sausage
2 TBS. olive oil
2 cups tomato sauce

1 tsp. oregano
1 cup chablis wine
1 lb. mushrooms, fresh and sliced

Sauté Italian sausage for a few minutes in olive oil—just long enough to seal it or firm it up. Remove sausage and let cool. Cut into bite-size pieces. Mix the rest of the ingredients in the skillet. Bring to a boil. Add sausage and cook for 1 hour on low heat.

Serve as a hot appetizer.

OYSTERS ED

¾ lb. mushrooms, thinly sliced
1½ sticks butter
3 or 4 TBS. plain flour
4 TBS. green onions—chop 'em
    up fine
2 cloves of garlic, minced

3 TBS. parsley (mince it up)
1½ tsp. of salt (1 is enough)
Dash of cayenne pepper
1/3 cup dry sherry
4 dozen oysters, drained dry
Bread crumbs

Sauté mushrooms in a couple or three tablespoons of butter. In a heavy pot, take the rest of the butter and all the flour and make a roux. Add the green onions, garlic, and parsley and cook the mixture down about 5 minutes or so. Take a beer break. Add the salt and cayenne and stir in the sherry. Now add the mushrooms and oysters and simmer about 5 to 10 minutes. Now put all this in individual ramekins and top with bread crumbs. Cook in oven at about 350 degrees for 15 minutes or until it's real hot. Now eat it!

CRABBY MUSHROOMS

1 cup crab meat
1 TBS. bread crumbs
1 TBS. minced onion
1 TBS. grated Parmesan cheese
1 tsp. salt

2 TBS. minced parsley
12 large mushrooms—remove
    stems and chop them fine
1 egg, beaten
Louisiana hot sauce, to taste

In a bowl, mix crab meat, bread crumbs, onions, cheese, salt, parsley, and chopped mushroom stems. Add beaten egg and hot sauce, to taste. Stuff mixture into mushroom caps. Bake at 300 degrees until tender, 15 to 30 minutes.

Serve it hot.

TASSO

Slice tasso very thinly with a sharp knife. Serve with beer on a warm afternoon. Tasso is like potato chips—you have to keep eating it. You can eat tasso with crackers, also, too.

Tasso is smoked seasoned meat that is used for flavoring other foods. It has no water added and usually has a coating of cayenne pepper and other seasoning on the outside.

TASSO PIZZA ON FRENCH BREAD

French bread
Olive oil
Spaghetti sauce, commercial or
   your own specialty
Romano cheese, grated

Tasso, sliced thin
Swiss cheese, grated
Pimento-stuffed olives
Any other toppings, like onions,
   peppers, mushrooms

Cut french bread into slices about ¾ inch thick. With a small kitchen brush, coat one side of bread with olive oil. Spoon on spaghetti sauce, but not too thick. Sprinkle with grated Romano cheese. Lay tasso slices on top. Sprinkle with more Romano cheese. Put on grated Swiss cheese. Put olives and other toppings on top. Sprinkle with a little more cheese.

Bake in a 250-degree oven for 30 minutes. Serve hot or cold.

Louisiana has all kind of fair and festival: crab, crawfish, shrimp, rice, gumbo, alligator, catfish, oyster, andouille, fur, strawberry, peach, soybean, watermelon, sauce piquant, cotton, and many udders. But you can be sure dat we got some pretty girls to go along wit' all our festivals.

BOILED PEANUTS

Salt
2 lbs. freshly dug peanuts
Water

Make a salty brine. Bring to a boil. Put peanuts in the brine. Boil for about an hour. Drain peanuts. You can put a little red cayenne pepper in with the salt if you would like, as some of us Cajuns do.

Serve warm.

Don' tole me you can't get fresh peanuts. I know from personal experiment dat dose North Louisianans from Detroits, Mitchigan, can grow peanuts in dere own garden.

Salads

Executive Cook's Salad
Sadie's Shrimp Salad
Artichoke Salad
Cucumber and Onion Salad
Picnic Potato Salad
Mos' Nilly Guacamole
Cole Slaw
Tomato and Onion Salad
No-Name-Yet Salad
Crawfish and Egg Salad
Justin's Tuna Salad
Mirliton Salad with Roquefort Dressing
Green Salad with Romano Cheese
Tuna and Avocado Salad
Catfish and Crawfish Mold

This is a cook's salad, not a chef's salad, no. And I was hungry when I made it, too.

EXECUTIVE COOK'S SALAD

Dressing:

1 clove garlic	2 tsp. Lea & Perrins
1 TBS. salt	Worcestershire sauce
½ cup olive oil	2 TBS. wine vinegar
2 tsp. Louisiana hot sauce or ¼	2 TBS. lemon juice
tsp. ground red pepper	

Salad ingredients:

Tasso	Mushrooms
Greens	Cheeses—cheddar and Swiss, and
Tomatoes, sliced	feta or Roquefort (optional)
Onions	Bell peppers

Anythings else you want to add—that's eatable, that is.

In a large wooden bowl, mash garlic with salt to a gritty paste. Add olive oil and stir well. Add the other dressing ingredients one at a time and stir after each. Slice tasso in thin strips, also mushrooms, onions, and bell peppers. Crumble feta cheese or Roquefort, if used. Slice cheddar and Swiss in thin slices. We don't tell you how much greens, tomatoes, onions, mushrooms, and bell pepper, but this will make a large salad. The tasso is to be used in rather small quantities.

Please note that an executive cook (namely I) and not a chef made this salad.

SADIE'S SHRIMP SALAD

2 lbs. macaroni, cooked

4 lbs. shrimp, boiled and peeled
 (yields 2-2½ lbs. shrimp)

2 dozen hard-boiled eggs,
 chopped

2 cups finely chopped onion

1 cup finely chopped celery

2 cups finely chopped black olives

2 cups chopped dill pickles

Dressing:

1 quart mayonnaise

½ cup olive oil

2 TBS. Louisiana hot sauce or ½
 tsp. ground red pepper

2 TBS. lemon juice

1 TBS. Lea & Perrins
 Worcestershire sauce

1 TBS. mustard

2 TBS. ketchup

Cook macaroni, drain, and cool. In a large bowl, mix macaroni, shrimp, eggs, onions, celery, olives, and pickles and toss well. Make dressing out of mayonnaise, olive oil, hot sauce, lemon juice, Worcestershire sauce, and mustard, and ketchup. Pour over other ingredients and mix well. Refrigerate 1 hour before serving. You may have to make more dressing if the salad takes it up.

Serves 30 people for a real picnic or party.

It's good! I garontee! And Sadie is my mother-in-law.

ARTICHOKE SALAD

4 fresh artichoke hearts
2 cans artichoke hearts, quartered
1 small clove garlic
2 tsp. salt
3 TBS. olive oil
1 TBS. lemon juice

1 TBS. wine vinegar
1 tsp. Louisiana hot sauce
 (cayenne pepper hot sauce)
1 tsp. Lea & Perrins
 Worcestershire sauce

In a wooden salad bowl, mash garlic and salt with a strong fork. Add fresh artichoke hearts, and mash with the garlic and salt. Add olive oil, stir, add lemon juice, stir, add wine vinegar, stir, add hot sauce, stir, add Worcestershire sauce. Mix well. Put canned artichoke hearts in dressing and let marinate for 1 hour, then eat as is or serve on a bed of greens.
 Serves 10.

CUCUMBER AND ONION SALAD

Dressing:

4 TBS. olive oil
1 TBS. wine vinegar
Louisiana hot sauce, to taste
2 TBS. lime juice

2 tsp. Lea & Perrins
 Worcestershire sauce
½ tsp. garlic powder
2 tsp. salt

Greens:

Cucumbers, sliced—enough for
 this dressing

Onions, sliced into thin rings—
 enough for this dressing

Mix ingredients for salad dressing really well. Add onions first then cucumbers and toss. Let set 20 minutes in dressing before serving.

You can tole dat I'm going on a picque-nique. I got my potato salad already made.

PICNIC POTATO SALAD

10 lbs. potatoes
8 or 7 hard-boiled eggs, chopped
2 cups dill relish
1 cup sweet relish
2 cups salad olives, chopped
2 cups finely chopped onions

1 cup finely chopped celery
1 cup finely chopped fresh parsley
1½ pints mayonnaise
½ cup yellow mustard
Salt, to taste
Louisiana hot sauce, to taste

Boil potatoes in their jackets. Let cool then peel and chop in large chunks. Mix mayonnaise, yellow mustard, Louisiana hot sauce, and salt together. Add to potatoes, along with the rest of the ingredients, and mix well. You can make this the day before and refrigerate it overnight. You may need to put a little more dressing on it if it is a little dry.

Serves 8 Cajuns or 24 other peoples for a good picnic.

MOS' NILLY GUACAMOLE

1 large avocado
1 clove garlic
1 TBS. salt
2 TBS. olive oil
1 TBS. lemon juice
2 TBS. wine vinegar
2 tsp. Louisiana hot sauce
   (cayenne pepper hot sauce)

2 tsp. Lea & Perrins
   Worcestershire sauce
4 oz. feta cheese
1 TBS. poupon mustard or creole-
   style mustard
¾ cup chopped parsley or cilantro
1 cup chopped tomatoes
Lettuce, as a bed for serving

Mash garlic with salt to make a gritty paste. Add avocado and mash some more. Pour lemon juice over avocado so that it will keep its color. Stir well. Add olive oil, stir, add Louisiana Hot sauce, stir, add Lea & Perrins, stir, and add wine vinegar. Stir. Add mustard. Stir. Crumble a good quantity of feta cheese in the dressing. Add chopped tomatoes and parsley. Stir well and serve over lettuce. This is also good for dipping.

Makes about 3 cups.

COLE SLAW

Dressing:

5 heaping TBS. mayonnaise
2 heaping TBS. yellow mustard
2 TBS. olive oil
1 TBS. wine vinegar
1 TBS. Lea & Perrins
  Worcestershire sauce

1 tsp. Louisiana hot sauce
  (cayenne pepper hot sauce)
2 TBS. ketchup
½ to 1 tsp. garlic salt
Juice of 1 medium-sized lemon
3 tsp. salt (or to taste)

Greens:

4 bell peppers, sliced
1 large head of cabbage, shredded

2 medium onions, shredded thin

Put mayonnaise and mustard in a bowl large enough to hold complete mixture, but shaped so that the mixture can be beaten with a fork. Beat mayonnaise and mustard until combined. Add olive oil slowly, beating all the time. Beat until mixture has returned to thickness of original mayonnaise. Add Louisiana hot sauce, continuing to beat. Add ketchup and keep beating. Add salt and garlic salt, beating all the time. Add wine vinegar (this will thin the sauce down). Beat this thoroughly, adding the lemon juice as you do so. Taste for salt and pepper. Place shredded cabbage, peppers, and onions in a large salad bowl. Pour sauce over and toss well. This should be done about an hour before serving.

Serves 10 people. Tastes better the next day.

TOMATO AND ONION SALAD

3 large ripe tomatoes, sliced
2 medium onions, sliced
1 large bell pepper, sliced
3 TBS. olive oil
1 TBS. wine vinegar

1 tsp. Louisiana hot sauce
  (cayenne pepper hot sauce)
1 TBS. lemon or lime juice
Salt, to taste
½ tsp. garlic powder

Slice tomatoes, onions, and bell pepper to make rings. Mix the other ingredients on the side and pour over vegetables. Let set about 15 minutes so they soak up the juices good. Some people like their dressing a little more tart, so you can add more wine vinegar for them.

Dis is so good, it should be against da law. I love to sop up da juice wid' toast, or biscuit, or bread, or cracker, or anyt'ing dat will sop.

NO-NAME-YET SALAD

1 16 oz. can peeled tomatoes, drained, (reserve juice)
3 or 4 hard-boiled eggs, chopped
1 6½ oz. can tuna, mashed or chopped with a fork
½ cup chopped onion
½ tsp. celery seed
2 TBS. of juice from drained tomatoes
2 TBS. dill relish

Chop tomatoes. Mix all of the above well. Add sauce. If it is too soupy, add some crushed saltine crackers.

Sauce:

2 heaping TBS. mayonnaise
2 heaping tsp. poupon or creole mustard
1 TBS. olive oil
2 tsp. Louisiana hot sauce (cayenne pepper hot sauce)
1 TBS. Lea & Perrins Worcestershire sauce
¼ tsp. garlic powder
Salt, to taste
2 tsp. wine vinegar

Beat mayonnaise and mustard really well, adding olive oil. Every time you add something, beat. Add all ingredients and beat hell out of them. Add to salad.

CRAWFISH AND EGG SALAD

3 hard-boiled eggs
1 lb. chopped crawfish or shrimp meat, cooked
2 TBS. finely chopped dill pickles
1 tsp. poupon mustard
1 TBS. Durkee's Famous Sauce
2 TBS. mayonnaise
Salt, if needed
½ to 1 tsp. red cayenne pepper

To cook crawfish:
In a saucepan bring 2 quarts water to boil with 2 tsp. salt and ½ tsp. of red pepper. Add peeled crawfish tails to water. Bring back to boil and remove from heat immediately. Drain and cool.

Chop hard-boiled eggs. Chop crawfish and mix with eggs. Add pickles. Mix mustard, Durkee's, and mayonnaise and add to egg mixture. If needed, add more pepper and salt.

Ricky French and me at de L.U.S. football game in our salad daze.

JUSTIN'S TUNA SALAD

3 hard-boiled eggs, chopped fine
2 heaping TBS. dill relish or
    chopped pickles
2 tsp. poupon mustard

2 TBS. mayonnaise
1 tsp. Louisiana hot sauce (or
    ground cayenne pepper)
1 6½ oz. can tuna, drained

Combine eggs and dill relish. Add the rest of the ingredients, except tuna, and mix really well. Then add tuna. If the mixture is dry, add some more mayonnaise.

This is fine for a sandwich.

Serves 8 people.

Sneak a little on crackers before dinner. GOOD!

MIRLITON SALAD
WITH ROQUEFORT DRESSING

Raw or cooked mirliton, sliced
    and arranged on a bed of
    lettuce.
1 TBS. lime juice
2 TBS. olive oil
4 TBS. mayonnaise

2 tsp. salt
1 TBS. wine vinegar
4 TBS. sour cream
Red pepper—just a sprinkling
Roquefort cheese—as much as
    you like

Beat olive oil into mayonnaise. Add lime juice and vinegar, salt, and red pepper, stirring constantly. Add sour cream, and then add the Roquefort cheese. Mix well and spoon over mirliton.

Peoples axe me "What is a mirliton?" It is a vegetable that grows on a vine. Sometimes it is called a vegetable pear or chayote. Whatever it is called, it's damned good, I garontee—whooooo boy.

GREEN SALAD
WITH ROMANO CHEESE

1 small clove garlic
4 anchovy fillets or 2 tsp. anchovy
   paste
1 TBS. salt
½ cup olive oil
1 TBS. Lea & Perrins
   Worcestershire sauce

2 tsp. Louisiana hot sauce
   (cayenne pepper hot sauce)
1 TBS. lime or lemon juice
2 TBS. wine vinegar
Assorted salad greens
Grated Romano cheese

   The amount of ingredients you use is determined by the amount of salad you want to make. This dressing can be stored if you make it ahead. With a strong dinner fork, mash garlic together with salt until a gritty paste is made. Add anchovies and mash well. Add olive oil, stir, add hot sauce, stir, add Worcestershire sauce, stir, add lime or lemon juice, add vinegar, stir.

   Tear greens into bite-sized pieces, and toss with dressing. Just before serving, sprinkle salad with Romano cheese.

   Serves 10 people.

TUNA AND AVOCADO SALAD

2 large hard-boiled eggs
1 cup mashed avocado
½ cup chopped onion
1 6½ oz. can tuna packed in water
2 TBS. dill relish or finely
   chopped dill pickles
Salt, to taste

Louisiana hot sauce, to taste
   (cayenne pepper hot sauce—
   about 2 tsp.)
Mayonnaise (about 2 to 3 TBS.)
Lemon juice to put on avocado to
   keep from discoloring

   Peel eggs and mash real well with a regular dinner fork (more or less mince them). Peel avocado and squeeze ½ lemon on it to keep from discoloring. Then mash real well with fork. Mix these two ingredients real well. Drain water from tuna and mix with onions, eggs, avocado, dill pickles or relish, salt, Louisiana hot sauce, and mayonnaise. Serve over lettuce.

   Serves 4 people.

CATFISH AND CRAWFISH MOLD

1 cup chopped parsley
½ cup dry white wine
1 TBS. lemon juice
1 tsp. Louisiana hot sauce
  (cayenne pepper hot sauce)
1 TBS. Lea & Perrins
  Worcestershire sauce

1 cup (8 oz.) cream cheese
Salt, to taste
1 lb. catfish meat, cooked
1 lb. crawfish meat, cooked

Chop catfish and crawfish in food processor. Add wine, parsley, lemon juice, and salt. Mix real well. Add hot sauce and Lea & Perrins Worcestershire sauce. Mix well. Add cream cheese. Mix well. Refrigerate overnight in a mold. Serve with crackers or on a bed of lettuce.

You can use shrimp if crawfish aren't available.

Pickled peppers add flavor and color to our table.

Sauces

Remoulade Sauce
Lisa's Tartar Sauce
Sauce for Raw Oysters
Dehydrator Barbecue Sauce
Marinade and Basting Sauce for Brisket of Beef
Beer Marinade for Beef
Barbecue Sauce
Barbecue Sauce au Justin
All-Purpose Marinade
Marinade for Lamb or Goat
Fish Marinade
Comforting Barbecue Sauce
Sauce for Boiled Crabs
Pepper Vinegar

REMOULADE SAUCE

1 pint mayonnaise
1 10 oz. bottle Durkee's Famous
    Sauce
¼ cup olive oil
1 cup (8 oz.) creole or poupon
    mustard
½ cup prepared horseradish

1 cup ketchup
2 TBS. wine vinegar
2 TBS. Lea & Perrins
    Worcestershire sauce
2 tsp. Louisiana hot sauce
    (cayenne pepper hot sauce)
Salt, if needed

Mix mayonnaise and Durkee's Sauce. Pour in olive oil gradually. Beat as if you are making mayonnaise. Add creole or poupon mustard, beat some more. Add horseradish, ketchup, wine vinegar, Lea & Perrins, and Louisiana hot sauce, beating after each ingredient. Pour over shrimp on salad or use as a sandwich sauce.

Some of my friends say they even like this over some desserts, but I don't believe them, no.

LISA'S TARTAR SAUCE

4 cups mayonnaise
1 cup sweet relish, chopped and
    drained
1 cup chow chow (sour), drained
1 bunch green onions, chopped
    fine (about 1 cup)
1 small to medium onion,
    chopped fine (about ½ to ¾ cup)

1 bunch parsley, chopped fine
    (about 1 cup)
Dash Lea & Perrins
    Worcestershire sauce
Dash Louisiana hot sauce
    (cayenne pepper hot sauce)

Mix all ingredients well and refrigerate overnight for best flavor. This can be used on all seafood. Tastes good also, too.
Sauce can be stored in the refrigerator for some time.

SAUCE FOR RAW OYSTERS

2 to 3 cups ketchup
4 heaping tsp. prepared
   horseradish
1 TBS. Louisiana hot sauce
   (cayenne pepper hot sauce)

8 oz. poupon mustard
3 TBS. lemon juice
2 cups finely chopped parsley
2 tsp. salt (or to taste)

Mix ingredients together, stirring after each ingredient is added. This makes about a quart. This is a basic red sauce for cooked and raw seafood.

DEHYDRATOR BARBECUE SAUCE

1 cup dehydrated onions
¼ cup dehydrated sweet peppers
¼ cup dried parsley
1 TBS. salt
½ tsp. dried mint
1 cup dry white wine
3 TBS. vinegar
1 cup water

1 cup ketchup
2 TBS. Louisiana hot sauce or 1½
   tsp. cayenne pepper
½ cup honey
1 TBS. lemon juice
3 TBS. Worcestershire sauce
1 TBS. Liquid Smoke

Put all the dried ingredients in a pot and add the water. Let it set a little while. Add the wine and the rest of the ingredients. Cover and cook for several hours. I use a food dehydrator to preserve vegetables when they are in season, then I store them and use them when I need them.

We let the meat fais do-do (sleep) in this sauce. Then we baste the meat with the same sauce that it sleep in.

We do this so when the meat is did it is healt'y and tasty and ready to eat.

46

MARINADE AND BASTING SAUCE
FOR BRISKET OF BEEF

———◆———

3 cups dry red wine	3 tsp. salt
1 cup olive or peanut oil	3 TBS. poupon mustard
2 TBS. wine vinegar	2 TBS. prepared horseradish
2 tsp. onion powder	3 TBS. lime juice
1 tsp. garlic powder	2 tsp. ground cayenne pepper

Mix all of the ingredients really well and then pour over whole beef brisket. Let marinate for several hours or overnight if possible. Also, use this marinade as a basting sauce.

BEER MARINADE FOR BEEF

———◆———

2 cans beer, fat or skinny (12 oz. or 10 oz. cans)	2 tsp. salt
½ cup olive oil	1 TBS. creole mustard
1 TBS. wine vinegar	1 tsp. ground cayenne pepper
1 tsp. onion powder	1 TBS. prepared horseradish
1 tsp. garlic powder	2 TBS. lemon juice

Mix all ingredients together and use as a marinade. Then use as a basting sauce for the meat while it cooks.

BARBECUE SAUCE

3 cups chopped onion
1 TBS. chopped garlic
1 cup chopped sweet pepper
½ cup dried parsley
1 cup dry white wine
3 TBS. vinegar
2 cups ketchup
½ TBS. Louisiana hot sauce or ¼
   tsp. ground cayenne pepper

¼ cup honey
2 TBS. lemon juice
1 TBS. salt
3 TBS. Worcestershire sauce
½ tsp. dried mint
1 TBS. Liquid Smoke

Place all ingredients in a pot that is big enough to hold them. Bring to a boil. Cook, covered, on low heat for several hours.

BARBECUE SAUCE AU JUSTIN

2 cups chopped onion
½ cup chopped bell pepper
½ cup olive oil
2 TBS. chopped garlic
1½ cups dry red wine
½ tsp. celery seed
1 cup steak sauce

¼ to ½ cup wine vinegar
4 tsp. salt
¼ cup Louisiana hot sauce or ½
   tsp. ground cayenne pepper
2 cups ketchup
2 TBS. dried parsley
2 TBS. lemon juice

Sauté onions and bell pepper in olive oil. Add garlic, wine, and the rest of the ingredients. Bring to a boil. Cover, then cook over a low fire for at least 2 hours. Use on finished barbecue, not as a basting sauce.

ALL-PURPOSE MARINADE

3 cups dry white wine
1 tsp. onion powder
½ tsp. garlic powder

½ tsp. cayenne pepper
½ cup soy sauce

Mix all the ingredients together. Marinate the meat (beef, pork, chicken, or game) for 3 to 6 hours, then use the marinade as a basting sauce as the meat cooks on the grill.

MARINADE FOR LAMB OR GOAT

4 cups chablis wine
1 cup green crème de menthe
1 TBS. onion powder
2 tsp. garlic powder
1 tsp. dried mint crushed into a
    powder (nearly)

2 TBS. Louisiana hot sauce or ½
    tsp. ground cayenne pepper
1 cup soy sauce
1 cup water (to rinse out
    measuring cup)
2 TBS. olive oil

Mix all the ingredients. Marinate lamb or goat 6 to 12 hours, then use the marinade as a basting sauce as it cooks.

FISH MARINADE

2 cups chablis wine
2 TBS. lemon juice
2 tsp. salt

2 TBS. creole mustard
½ tsp. ground cayenne pepper

Mix all the ingredients together and stir well. Use as a marinade, then as a basting sauce when you cook fish.

COMFORTING BARBECUE SAUCE

4 cups chopped onion
1 cup chopped celery
1 cup chopped bell pepper
1 cup chopped fresh parsley
1 cup peanut cooking oil
2 TBS. chopped garlic

3 cups steak sauce
½ cup Louisiana hot sauce or 2
   tsp. ground cayenne pepper
3 cups ketchup
3 tsp. salt or to taste
1 cup Southern Comfort liquor

In a large skillet, sauté onions, celery, bell pepper and parsley in peanut oil until onions are clear or tender. Add garlic and cook a little longer. Add steak sauce, hot sauce, and ketchup. Salt to taste. Add Southern Comfort. Bring to a boil. Lower heat and cover. Cook for 2 to 3 hours. This sauce can be stored in the refrigerator for several weeks.

Makes 3 quarts to 1 gallon.

This is not to drink, no. It's to use as a bubba-que sauce, but it also, too, is mighty fine for soppin'.

SAUCE FOR BOILED CRABS

2 TBS. Lea & Perrins
  Worcestershire sauce
1 TBS. creole or poupon mustard
1 cup ketchup
1 heaping tsp. prepared
  horseradish

1 cup finely chopped parsley
1 tsp. Louisiana hot sauce or a little ground cayenne pepper
Juice of 1 lemon
Salt, to taste

Mix all of the ingredients together, beating after each addition. Pour mixture over cooked crab meat or shrimp as for a seafood cocktail.

PEPPER VINEGAR

Peppers—fresh from the garden
Vinegar

Salt to taste
Water

Pack peppers and salt in a jar that has a rubber or plastic lid. Metal lids will disintegrate. Combine 1 part water and 4 parts vinegar and heat until it's too hot to leave your finger in it. Pour liquid into jar over peppers, covering all of them. Seal jar and turn upside down. The peppers don't know which end is up. This pepper vinegar is used all over the South on greens and beans and to make all sorts of foods taste good.

Soups and Gumbos

Shrimp and Corn Soup
Gizzard Gumbo with Andouille
Fish Courtbouillion au Justin
Oyster and Andouille Gumbo
Oyster Artichoke Soup
Filé
Chicken Andouille Gumbo
Shrimp Soup
Vegetable Soup

Andouille sausage is used in gumbo, vegetables, and jus' plain. It's got a flavor like nothing else.

SHRIMP AND CORN SOUP

6 cups water
1 cup dry white wine
½ tsp. cayenne pepper
Salt, to taste
1 cup finely chopped onion
2 cups chopped or mashed
   tomatoes

½ cup finely chopped parsley
½ TBS. finely chopped garlic
2 cups whole kernel corn
1 lb. shrimp, chopped

Put water, wine, pepper, and some salt in a pot large enough to hold everything. Bring to a boil. Add onions, tomatoes, parsley, garlic, and corn. Bring back to a boil. Then lower heat to a simmer and add shrimp. Cook on low heat for one hour stirring occasionally.
   Serves 10.

GIZZARD GUMBO WITH ANDOUILLE

1 cup bacon drippings or cooking
   oil (for roux)
2 cups plain flour (for roux)
½ cup chopped bell pepper
1 cup chopped parsley
1½ cup chopped green onions
½ cup chopped celery
2 large onions, chopped fine
8 cups water
Salt, to taste

3 TBS. Lea & Perrins
   Worcestershire sauce
1 TBS. Louisiana hot sauce
   (cayenne pepper hot sauce)
1 large clove garlic, chopped fine
4 cups dry white wine
4 lbs. gizzards
1 lb. andouille sausage, cut into
   ¼-inch slices

First, you make a roux. (See my recipe.) Add all of the vegetables to the roux and cook until the onions are clear. Add 2 cups cold water. Stir until everything is well mixed. Add the rest of the water, salt, seasonings, and wine. Then add the gizzards and andouille. Cover and bring to a boil. Put on low heat and simmer for 3 or 4 hours. Sprinkle filé on rice in a bowl and serve.
   This is so good, my stomach just can't stand too much of it axcept every day.

FISH COURTBOUILLION AU JUSTIN

4 cups chopped onion
1 cup chopped celery
1 cup chopped bell pepper
3 **TBS.** olive oil
2 cups chopped parsley
3 cups chopped green onions
1 **TBS.** chopped garlic
1 cup grated carrots
12 cups water
¼ cup lemon juice
2 cups dry (white) wine

8 to 10 cups fish, skinned and boned and cut in large pieces. *You can use the head too, but take the eyes out.*
2 **TBS.** Lea & Perrins Worcestershire sauce
1 **TBS.** soy sauce
1 **TBS.** Louisiana hot sauce (cayenne pepper hot sauce)
6 tsp. salt, or to taste

In large heavy pot, sauté onions, celery, and bell pepper in olive oil until tender or clear. Add parsley, green onions, garlic, and carrots. Add water and simmer about 15 minutes. Pour in lemon juice, wine, fish, and the remainder of the ingredients. Cover and bring to a boil and let cook on low heat (nearly simmer) for 3 to 4 hours. Do not stir because you don't want to break up the fish. The pot can be picked up and rotated slightly, however.

Serves a whole bunch of people, maybe 20.

OYSTER AND ANDOUILLE GUMBO

½ cup of olive oil (for roux)
1 to 1½ cups plain flour (for roux)
2 cups chopped onion
½ cup chopped bell pepper
1 cup chopped parsley
½ tsp. ground cayenne pepper

1 **TBS.** minced garlic
4 cups water
2 cups dry white wine
1 lb. andouille, sliced ¼ inch thick
1 quart oysters, with juice

Make a roux (see my recipe). After roux is dark brown, add onions and bell pepper. Cook until tender, watching carefully to keep from burning roux. Add parsley and garlic. Add some cold water and stir to bring roux to a smooth paste. Add more water and the wine. Bring to a boil and add andouille. Cover and bring back to a boil. Cut heat back and cook at medium heat for about 1 hour. Add oysters and their juice. Cut heat to simmer. Simmer for 30 minutes. Do not boil after oysters have been added.

Sprinkle filé over rice and serve in a bowl. Should serve 8 to 10.

OYSTER ARTICHOKE SOUP

8 cups water
1 cup chablis wine
2 tsp. Louisiana hot sauce or ½
   tsp. ground cayenne pepper
Salt, to taste
1 cup chopped onion

¼ cup finely chopped celery
½ tsp. chopped garlic
1 cup finely chopped parsley
4 cups canned artichoke hearts,
   drained
4 cups oysters and juice

Put water and wine in large pot. Add hot sauce or pepper, some of salt, onion, garlic, and parsley. Cook this for about 20 to 30 minutes. Add artichoke hearts, cover, and bring to a boil. Cut fire down to simmer and add oysters. Simmer for about 30 to 45 minutes. Do not boil after oysters have been added.

Should serve 8 to 10 people that are not too hungry.

This is a popular before-dinner soup in South Louisiana.

FILÉ

In South Louisiana we use filé on gumbo and soups after they are cooked and when they are served. Filé has a delicate flavor and also thickens the liquid to which it is added.

Filé is made from the leaves of the sassafras tree. At the end of summer, in the second or third week of September, we gather the leaves. Sometimes small branches are cut off and sometimes just the leaves are picked from the trees. Then the leaves are cleaned and left to dry in the sun.

After the leaves are thoroughly dried we take the big spines off by stripping the leaves. Then we either pound them in a heavy canvas sack or put them in a blender to make a green powder. This is filé.

John Folse is a fine chef. He came by to help me stir a chicken andouille gumbo.

Charlie Johnson is my chief taster. He doesn't only help me stir, he also helps me eat.

CHICKEN ANDOUILLE GUMBO

1 cup bacon drippings or cooking oil (for roux)
2 cups plain flour (for roux)
1 baking hen with fat
4 cups chopped onion
½ cup chopped bell pepper
½ cup chopped celery
1 TBS. chopped garlic
2 cups chopped parsley
8 to 10 cups water
1 cup chopped green onions
4 TBS. Lea & Perrins Worcestershire sauce
1 TBS. Louisiana hot sauce or 1 tsp. ground cayenne pepper
4 cups dry white wine
½ tsp. dried mint
2 lbs. andouille, cut into ¼-inch slices
Salt, to taste

Brown chicken using chicken fat. Make a dark roux (see my recipe). Add onions, bell pepper, and celery. Cook until onions are clear or tender. Add garlic and parsley. Let cook a few minutes. Add 3 or 4 cups of water. Stir until everything is well mixed or smooth. Add everything except chicken. Mix real well. Add browned off chicken and andouille. Taste for salt, some more may be needed. Cover and bring to a boil, then lower to simmer and cook for 4 or 3 hours stirring occasionally.

Serve over rice and filé in a bowl.

SHRIMP SOUP

8 cups chicken stock
1 cup chopped green onions
½ cup chopped celery
1 TBS. diced garlic
1 cup chopped parsley
2 cups dry white wine
2 tsp. Louisiana hot sauce or ½ tsp. ground cayenne pepper
Salt, to taste
1 TBS. Lea & Perrins Worcestershire sauce
2 lbs. shrimp, chopped

Put ingredients except shrimp in chicken stock. Bring to a boil and then lower heat. Cover, and cook for 45 minutes. Add shrimp and simmer for 30 minutes more.

VEGETABLE SOUP

Water—enough to cover all
    ingredients
Beef ribs
Louisiana hot sauce or cayenne
    pepper, to taste
Worcestershire sauce, to taste
Salt, to taste
Onions, chopped
Garlic, chopped
Parsley, chopped

Turnips or fresh potatoes, cubed
Tomatoes, fresh or canned,
    chopped
Carrots, shredded
Green beans, cut
Cabbage, shredded
Lima beans
And anything else you have on
    hand

How long is a piece of string? How big a pot of vegetable soup do you wish to make? See what you have in the pantry and then figure out your soup. There are certain "Musts" though. These are onions, garlic, tomatoes, and ribs (you can use brisket, but I find ribs better).

Put water in a pot (big enough) with beef ribs (or whatever you have). Water should cover beef by about 1 or 2 inches. Then add pepper, Worcestershire sauce and salt. Add onions, garlic, parsley, potatoes or turnips, and tomatoes. Look in your pantry and add whatever you have. DO NOT ADD creamed corn—it sticks. Bring to a boil, then lower heat. Taste for salt and cook for 2 hours or more. Tastes better tomorrow.

I make this in the winter and eat it for a whole week or give part of it to my neighbors. Then the whole neighborhood is happy.

Breads

Hush Puppies
Corn Flour Bread
Hot Water Corn Bread
Fig Bread
Sweet Potato Bread
Garlic Bread on Grill
Buttermilk Bread
Couche-Couche
Tasso Toast
Easy Home Made Bread

Hush puppies ready to go . . .

. . . and goin'.

HUSH PUPPIES

2 cups cornmeal
1 cup plain flour
1 tsp. baking powder
1 tsp. salt
½ tsp. soda
½ cup finely chopped parsley
Garlic powder, to taste (about ½ tsp.)

Ground cayenne pepper, to taste
2 eggs, beaten
¾ to 1 cup buttermilk
1 cup finely chopped green onion
2 TBS. hot cooking oil or bacon drippings
Deep fat (oil) for frying

Combine all dry ingredients. Add eggs, buttermilk, onions, and oil or bacon drippings. Mix well. Drop in deep hot fat by spoonfuls and brown on all sides.

"Hush puppy" is an old Southern term that originated after the Civil War. People didn't have enough for themselves to eat let alone feed their dogs, so when the old hounds started barking from hunger, they would throw pieces of fried corn bread to them, yelling, "Shut up, dog! Hush, puppy!"

CORN FLOUR BREAD

3 **TBS.** shortening, melted in
    skillet or corn bread pan
2 cups corn flour
2 tsp. baking powder

1 tsp. salt
1½ cups milk or buttermilk
½ tsp. soda, if buttermilk is used
2 eggs, beaten well

In 400-degree oven, heat shortening in pan or skillet. Mix all dry ingredients well. Pour milk and beaten eggs into center of dry mixture. Mix very well. Pour hot shortening into mixture and beat. Pour mixture back into skillet or pan. Bake for 45 minutes at 400 degrees. Flip cornbread over. Cut oven off and place skillet back in oven for about 20 minutes.

Makes two 8-inch pans.

HOT WATER CORN BREAD

1 cup cornmeal
½ cup plain flour
1 tsp. salt

Boiling water
Cooking oil for deep frying

Blend the dry ingredients. Add boiling water to make a very stiff batter. Using a spoon, make small pieces and drop them into deep hot grease. Brown on all sides.

You can also roll this stiff batter in your hand and make a 2-inch-long piece to drop in deep oil.

Serves 6.

FIG BREAD

3 eggs
2½ cups sugar
2 cups ripe fresh figs, mashed
¾ cup peanut or salad oil
3 cups plain flour

2 tsp. baking soda
1 tsp. salt
½ tsp. cinnamon
½ cup buttermilk
1 cup chopped pecans

Beat eggs. Add sugar and beat well. Add fig purée and oil. Sift together flour, soda, salt, and cinnamon. Add to the fig mixture alternately with the buttermilk. Beat well. Fold in pecans. Bake at 350 degrees for 1 hour in greased and floured loaf pans.
Yields 3 loaves.

SWEET POTATO BREAD

4 cups sweet potatoes, cooked and
    mashed
2 cups warm milk
1 envelope yeast

3 TBS. oleo
3 cups plain flour, well sifted
2 eggs, beaten well
1 TBS. salt

Boil or bake sweet potatoes in their jackets. Peel and mash with a fork or use a food processor to make a purée.
In a large heavy bowl, combine warm milk and yeast. Add oleo, which will melt in warm milk. Beat well. Let set 1 hour for yeast to start working. Add eggs, salt, and potato purée, making sure that any large fibers have been removed. Add sifted flour and beat until the dough is light and spongy. Cover bowl with clean dish cloth. Set in a warm place for mixture to rise until double.
Turn on to floured surface and mold into loaves or use greased bread pans. Let rise until light. Bake in oven at 350 degrees for 45 minutes, or until done.

Here is sure proof that I'm executive cook at my house. I wash my own dishes.

GARLIC BREAD ON GRILL

French bread
Garlic purée
Oleo

Parmesan or Romano cheese
Parsley, dried
Black pepper

Cut french bread lengthwise. Mix oleo and garlic purée together. Spread oleo and garlic purée mixture on bread. Sprinkle with cheese, dried parsley, and black pepper.

Place on grill outside or under broiler and toast.

Watch it closely—toast burns with three people watching it, and easy, I garontee.

BUTTERMILK BREAD

1 tsp. soda
2 cups buttermilk
1 TBS. oleo or butter

½ cup powdered sugar
4 cups plain flour, sifted
1 tsp. salt

Dissolve soda in 2 TBS. warm water. Warm buttermilk and add to it soda, butter, and sugar. Pour into a large heavy bowl. Sift together flour and salt into bowl and mix wet and dry ingredients well. Leave to rise. When well risen, turn onto floured surface and knead lightly. Place in a greased baking pan. Let rise for ½ hour.

Bake at 350 degrees until brown. This is a slightly sweet, light white bread. Rolls can also be made by placing pieces about the size of a small egg on a sheet and baking.

COUCHE-COUCHE

½ cup oil   1½ tsp. salt
2 cups cornmeal   1½ cups milk

Heat oil in a heavy pot on stove. Mix cornmeal, salt, and milk. Stir well. Add corn mixture to oil. Stir. The mixture will be a little crusty. Lower heat and cover. Cook for 15 minutes, stirring occasionally.

Serve with cane syrup or more milk and sugar.

Cajun children grow up on couche-couche for breakfast. And after they are grown up, they still eat it.

TASSO TOAST

Bread, all kinds—bagels, white,   Tasso, sliced thin
    brown   Cheese, sliced thin
Mustard

Toast bread slightly. Spread one side with mustard. Lay tasso slices on top, then place cheese on top. Put on a pan under a broiler to melt cheese. Watch very carefully. Serve with eggs for a good breakfast.

EASY HOME MADE BREAD

2 cups warm water   1½ tsp. salt
1 package dry yeast   ¼ cup sugar
3 TBS. vegetable oil   4 to 5 cups flour

Mix all ingredients together using as much flour as is needed to make the dough elastic. Let dough rise until double in volume. Knead it just a little. Let it rise in a warm place until double again. Knead again and shape into loaves or rolls. Let rise until double again. Bake at 400 degrees until brown. Brush the tops with butter.

Makes 2 loaves or 2 small pans of rolls.

Seafood

How to Peel a Crawfish
Stuffed Shrimp
Rice and Oyster Dressing
Crab and Crawfish Etouffée
Squash and Crawfish
How to Crack a Crab
Oysters au Justin
Frogleg Etouffée
Crawfish or Shrimp Jambalaya
Embrochette Oysters and Bacon
Louisiana Oysters on Half Shell
Barbecued Oysters
Stuffed Crabs
Fish in Tomato Sauce on Barbecue Pit
Crawfish Boudin
Fish-Stuffed Bell Pepper
Boiled Crawfish
Shrimp with Caper Sauce
Barbecued Shrimp
Boiled Crabs
Fried Crawfish Tails
Deep-Fried Catfish
Deep-Fried Oysters
Boiled Shrimp
Deep-Fried Soft-Shelled Crab
Marinated Fried Fish Fillets
Crawfish Maque-Chou
Crawfish Pie
Oyster Rockefella Casserole

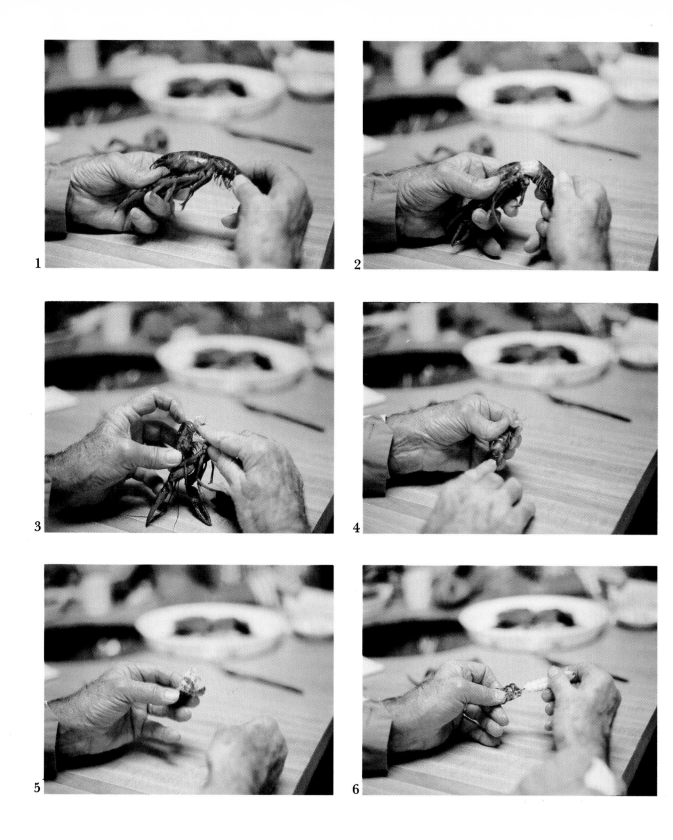

HOW TO PEEL A CRAWFISH

1. Hold the crawfish with its head in one hand, its tail in the other. The claws are pointed down.

2. Separate the head from the body. Pull the tail toward you and down. The two parts will separate easily.

3. Some people throw the head away, but they are missing a treat. I push my forefinger into the head where I get the bright yellow "fat." Other people suck the head to get the "fat" and taste the juices in which the crawfish were boiled. You can then throw the head away.

4. Squeeze the sides of the tail. With your thumb and forefinger, press the sides of the top of the tail. The shell will give and should crack.

5. Remove the first three segments of the tail. Peel the segments around and off.

6. Pull out the meat. Using your thumb and forefinger, pinch the tail just above the flippers at the last segment. Using your other thumb and forefinger, pull on the exposed meat. The whole tail section should come out. This is the part that is eaten.

STUFFED SHRIMP

15 large shrimp
1 cup very finely chopped onion
1 cup finely chopped parsley
2 cups crab meat (check all shell
  has been removed)
1 cup bread crumbs

2 large eggs
Salt
Cayenne pepper
Corn flour
Fat for deep frying
Oil

In a skillet sauté onions and parsley until tender. Add crab meat and bread crumbs. Mix well. Remove from heat. Beat one egg slightly. Mix with crab mixture. Add salt and cayenne, to taste. Mix well.

Select 15 large shrimp. Peel them, but leave the tails on. Slice down the back, but don't cut all the way through. Open the flesh out flat. Push stuffing inside the opening, then put the flaps back. Dust lightly with corn flour. Dip in egg wash made from the other egg. Coat with more corn flour or bread crumbs.

Deep fry at 365–375 degrees until light brown.

RICE AND OYSTER DRESSING

2 cups chopped green onions
½ cup chopped celery
1 cup chopped parsley
¼ cup oil or bacon drippings
3 cups cooked rice
1 pint medium-sized oysters (save
  liquid)

2 cups cooked giblets (no livers),
  chopped (save stock)
Salt, to taste
Louisiana hot sauce, to taste
  (cayenne pepper hot sauce)

Sauté green onions, celery, and parsley in oil until tender. Add cooked rice and mix well. Add oysters. Add giblets and oyster liquid and some of the giblet stock if needed. Add salt and pepper, to taste. Mix well in pan.

Bake in 350-degree oven for 30 to 40 minutes. Or stuff a duck, turkey, goose, or chicken and bake.

CRAB AND CRAWFISH ETOUFFÉE

½ lb. oleo
5 cups chopped onion (same in volume as crawfish and crab meat)
½ cup chopped bell pepper
3 cups chopped parsley
2 TBS. lemon juice

1½ TBS. Lea & Perrins Worcestershire sauce
1 tsp. Louisiana hot sauce (cayenne pepper hot sauce)
3 tsp. salt or to taste
1 lb. crab meat
2 lbs. crawfish meat with fat

Melt oleo in pot. Sauté onions, bell pepper, and parsley until tender. Simmer, covered for 30 to 40 minutes. Add lemon juice, Lea & Perrins, Louisiana hot sauce, and salt. Add crab meat and crawfish—be sure to use crawfish fat if you have it. Mix well, cover, and simmer for 30 minutes.

Serve over rice. Will feed 30 people.

Shrimp may be substituted for crawfish.

SQUASH AND CRAWFISH

3 cups chopped onion
½ cup chopped bell pepper
1 TBS. olive oil
2 cups water
1 TBS. chopped garlic
½ cup dried parsley flakes

12 cups cubed zucchini squash
2 cups chablis wine
3 TBS. salt (more if necessary)
2 to 3 tsp. Louisiana hot sauce (cayenne pepper hot sauce)
2 lbs. crawfish meat

Sauté onions and pepper in olive oil until tender. Add 1 cup of water. Add garlic and parsley. Simmer for 10 minutes, adding more water if necessary. Add squash, wine, water, salt, and Louisiana hot sauce. Simmer for 1 hour. Add crawfish and simmer for 15 minutes.

Feeds a dozen people.

9 10

HOW TO CRACK A CRAB

1. Hold the crab belly up. Pry under the shell with your fingers or with a knife along the "T" or triangular-shaped seam. Lift the center shape out.

2. Turn the crab over. Hold the crab firmly with one hand; with the other hand pull the top shell off. Remove the internal organs.

3. Take out the lungs, the tubular-shaped organs tht lie on the body of the crab.

4. Remove the mouth and eyes with a knife or your fingers.

5. Pull off the small legs and swimmerets. Some fine white meat may cling to these as they come out.

6. Remove the two large claws and set them aside.

7. Break the body in half. Carefully open the chambers that contain white meat on each half of the body. Remove the meat with your fingers or a knife. The meat from the largest chamber is called "lump" crab meat.

8. Crack the claws. With the moveable side down, saw lightly through the shell near the pincher using a small serrated knife.

9. Twist the knife slightly. The shell will crack cleanly all the way around.

10. Gently pull off the shell. There will be a large piece of claw meat with a handle for eating. Use the knife handle to crack the other joint of the claw. Claw meat is generally a little darker and coarser than white meat. The flavor is slightly different, too, but it's all very good.

When I eat boiled crabs I jes' get tired before I get full.

OYSTERS AU JUSTIN

½ gallon chopped onion
½ cup chopped bell pepper
3 cups chopped parsley
½ lb. oleo
1 TBS. Lea & Perrins
   Worcestershire sauce

1 TBS. Louisiana hot sauce
   (cayenne pepper hot sauce)
½ tsp. celery seed
Salt, to taste
3 drops bitters
½ gallon oysters (preserve juice)

Sauté onions, bell pepper, and parsley in oleo until onions are clear and tender. Add other seasonings, stirring after each ingredient. Add 1 cup of juice from oysters and stir. Bring to a boil. Add oysters. Then lower the heat and simmer for 1 hour. Do not boil after oysters have been added.

Serve over rice. Will feed 24 people.

This smells so good, you have to cook it outside. If you cook it inside, you will be hungry 3 weeks from now.

FROGLEG ETOUFFÉE

1 lb. oleo
4 cups chopped onion
½ cup chopped bell pepper
1 cup dried parsley flakes
Louisiana hot sauce, to taste
   (cayenne pepper hot sauce)

2 TBS. Lea & Perrins
   Worcestershire sauce
Salt, to taste
2 TBS. lemon juice
4 lbs. froglegs

Melt oleo in pot and then add onions, pepper, parsley, Louisiana hot sauce, Worcestershire sauce, salt, and lemon juice. Cover, and simmer for 1 hour. This will make its own juice. Add froglegs and cook, covered, for about 30 minutes to 1 hour on a low fire (simmer). Serve over rice.

Serves 12 or more people, depending on who is eating and how hungry they are.

CRAWFISH OR SHRIMP JAMBALAYA

2 cups chopped onion
1 cup chopped green onions
½ cup chopped bell pepper
2 TBS. bacon drippings
2 TBS. olive oil
1 cup chopped fresh mushrooms
Water
1 tsp. chopped garlic
2 TBS. chopped parsley
4 tsp. salt

2 cups chablis wine
1 TBS. Louisiana hot sauce
   (cayenne pepper hot sauce)
1 TBS. Lea & Perrins
   Worcestershire sauce
1 8 oz. can tomato sauce
4 cups rice
2 lbs. crawfish tails or peeled
   shrimp

Sauté onions and bell pepper in olive oil and bacon drippings. Add mushrooms and a little water. Then, add garlic, parsley, salt, wine, Louisiana hot sauce, Worcestershire sauce, and tomato sauce. Add rice and water to cover rice about 1 inch. Bring to a boil. Add crawfish or shrimp. Stir well. Cook on medium heat until most of the liquid is gone. Then cover and simmer about 1 hour. Don't open the lid until the hour is up.

Serves 12 to 15 people.

Some people put sugar in jambalaya to counteract the bitterness of the tomato sauce, but the wine will do the same thing. I like the wine much more better.

Jus' be careful when doing this. You see dat glove I got on my hand.

EMBROCHETTE OYSTERS AND BACON

Barbecue pit
Wood for smoking (pecan,
    hickory, cherry, oak, or
    mesquite)

Oysters
Thin-sliced bacon
Skewers

First, build your barbecue fire on one end of pit. When charcoal has all lighted, put some smoking wood that has been soaked in water on it to make it smoke. You do not want a fire or coals that are too hot.

While your fire is getting ready, wrap each oyster with thin-sliced bacon and put on a skewer. Do not let each wrapped oyster touch the other—keep them about ¼ to ½ inch apart. Place on barbecue pit away from fire for a few minutes. Then place where the fire is and sear for a short time. Remove and serve while hot.

I don't put amounts here because you make as much as you want. Use ½ slice bacon for each oyster and as many oysters as you can stand. I can stand about at least 1 dozen of these oysters in a pig blanket, myself.

LOUISIANA OYSTERS ON HALF SHELL

First of all, be sure that oysters are fresh and have not been off refrigeration very long.

There is a knife called an oyster knife that is best for opening oysters. If you don't have one, use a thick-bladed knife that is not too sharp.

I recommend that you use a cotton glove on the hand holding the oyster. Hold oyster down on a table or cutting board that is stable. About halfway from the thick end where the oyster hinges to the thin or other end, find a place where it is fairly easy to insert your knife. Remember that an oyster doesn't like for you to see it (him/her). When you get the knife inserted, twist until shell opens. With your knife, scrape the upper part of the shell where muscle of oyster is until oyster comes away from that shell. Clean all the shell away from oyster resting on shell. Be sure your knife is clean and go under oyster until it is free from shell. Place on tray of ice, or eat it right away.

You can dip in sauce, or I just squeeze lemon on oyster.

Louisiana oysters are the happiest oysters in the world, I garontee.

BARBECUED OYSTERS

Put foil on grill. Place oysters on foil, close lid, and smoke cook. Baste with marinade brush. You have to watch them closely because they cook very fast. When their edges curl slightly, they are done.

STUFFED CRABS

1 cup minced parsley
1 cup minced onion
2 TBS. minced garlic
4 TBS. oleo
2 lbs. catfish fillet
2 lbs. crab meat
2 cups water
4 eggs, beaten

3 cups bread crumbs
2 TBS. Louisiana hot sauce
 (cayenne pepper hot sauce)
2 TBS. Lea & Perrins
 Worcestershire sauce
1 tsp. dried mint, crushed
2 TBS. salt
1 cup chablis wine

Sauté parsley, onions, and garlic in oleo in a large skillet. Grind catfish and crab meat together in a food processor and add to sautéed vegetables. Add water, then eggs, bread crumbs, and then the rest of the seasonings, including the wine. Let this all cook for about 15 minutes, stirring frequently. Place in crab shells and bake in preheated 325-degree oven for approximately 15 to 20 minutes.

These can also be deep fried at 350 degrees for 3 to 5 minutes.

Wondermus! Wondermus! Depending on the size of your crab shells, this will stuff 18 to 24 crabs.

FISH IN TOMATO SAUCE
ON BARBECUE PIT

1 cup finely chopped onion
1 cup chopped parsley
2 TBS. olive oil or peanut oil
1 TBS. finely chopped garlic
4 cups peeled and chopped fresh
  tomatoes

Ground red pepper, to taste
Salt, to taste
2 cups burgundy wine
1 TBS. soy sauce
1 large fish (red snapper, redfish,
  or catfish)

Place onions and parsley in olive oil and sauté for a little while. Add garlic and then the rest of the ingredients except fish. Cook until the onions are nearly done. Pour sauce over fish to be baked on pit in a boat made from aluminum foil.

CRAWFISH BOUDIN

1 cup chopped onion
¼ cup oil
1 cup chopped parsley
1 cup water

2 lbs. crawfish tails, chopped
4 cups cooked rice
2 tsp. salt or to taste
Cayenne pepper, to taste

Sauté onions in oil until clear. Add parsley and cook 5 minutes. Add water and bring to a boil. Add crawfish and bring back to boil. Add rice, salt, and pepper. Cook 5 minutes. Let cool then use a sausage stuffer to stuff into natural casing.

When serving, heat in pan with a small amount of water until heated through. Actually, you are steaming the boudin.

Some of my friends cooked up a few crawfish. It took me almost an afternoon to eat my share.

FISH-STUFFED BELL PEPPER

4 cups fillet of fish, ground up
3 cups chopped green onions
1 cup chopped parsley
3 TBS. olive oil
2 cups dry white wine
2 tsp. chopped garlic
1 TBS. Louisiana hot sauce or ¼
    tsp. ground red pepper

2 TBS. soy sauce
Salt, to taste
2 TBS. chopped pepper
1 cup seasoned bread crumbs
8 large bell peppers
2 16 oz. cans tomato sauce

Grind fish or put through food processor. Sauté onions and parsley in olive oil. Add 1 cup wine, chopped garlic, Louisiana hot sauce, soy sauce, salt, and chopped pepper. Cook until onions and pepper are done or real tender. Let cool for a few minutes. In large mixing bowl, combine ground fish, sautéed ingredients, and bread crumbs. Stuff mixture into peppers. Place in baking pan. Mix 1 cup wine and tomato sauce and pour over all the peppers.

Bake at 350 degrees for approximately 1 hour to 1½ hours or until peppers are tender.

BOILED CRAWFISH

4 boxes salt
6 pouches crab boil
8 lemons
8 oz. cayenne pepper
Onions

Garlic
24 small potatoes
Smoked sausage
Corn
50 lbs. live crawfish

Bring seasonings to boil for about 10 minutes. Add potatoes, corn, and smoked sausage. Boil for another 10 minutes. Add crawfish. Bring back to boil. Cut fire off immediately. Let soak for 20 to 30 minutes. Drain. Peel and eat.

While water is coming to a boil, cull and clean crawfish. Rinse well with garden hose and remove any dead ones.

Always wear gloves when you fool with crawfish, but remember they can still pinch you through the gloves.

Not everybody likes the fat, but I do, and I love to dig my finger into the head and scoop it out. During crawfish season, my finger stays yellow from one end to the other.

SHRIMP WITH CAPER SAUCE

1 cup finely chopped onion
½ cup chopped parsley
½ cup olive oil
1 TBS. minced garlic
½ tsp. dried mint, crumbled
2 TBS. Worcestershire sauce

1 tsp. Louisiana hot sauce or ¼
   tsp. ground cayenne red pepper
Salt, to taste
1 cup chablis or dry white wine
2 lbs. shrimp, shelled and
   deveined

Sauce:

¾ cup mayonnaise
1 TBS. lemon juice
1 TBS. creole or poupon mustard

2 TBS. drained capers

Sauté onions and parsley in olive oil until tender. Add garlic, mint, Worcestershire sauce, hot sauce, salt, wine, and shrimp. Cook, stirring all the time, until shrimp are golden or red. To make sauce, combine mayonnaise, lemon juice, mustard, and capers. Mix real well. Serve shrimp over rice or spaghetti and top with sauce. Do not mix sauce with shrimp until you serve.

BARBECUED SHRIMP

Leave shrimp in shell. Baste with marinade and place on grill in foil and cook, basting frequently. You have to watch them closely because they cook very fast.

Serve with barbecue sauce.

BOILED CRABS

4 or 5 boxes salt—make nearly a
　brine
1 pod garlic, whole
8 onions, halved
8 lemons, halved

8 oz. cayenne pepper
6 bags crab boil
Water, to cover
3 or 4 dozen crabs

　　Bring seasonings to a boil. Let boil for 15 minutes. Add crabs. Let cook approximately 5 minutes or until they float. Cut fire off. Let crabs soak for about 15 minutes. Remove from water and cool. Crack and eat.

FRIED CRAWFISH TAILS

1 lb. peeled crawfish tails, raw
Oil for deep frying

Drench:

1 cup dry white wine
½ tsp. garlic powder
½ tsp. onion powder

½ tsp. ground cayenne pepper
1 tsp. salt

Dredge:

Corn flour mixed with salt and
　red cayenne pepper, to taste

　　Mix all of the above ingredients for drench together. Pass crawfish through and then put in dredge. Deep fry tails at 350 degrees for a minute until done.
　　You can use shrimp for this dish, but crawfish are better.

The second one will taste even better than the first one, I garontee!

Fried catfish is something we been eatin' in Louisiana for a long time. The reason? 'Cause it tastes good.

DEEP-FRIED CATFISH

The amounts of the ingredients you use are determined by the amount of fish you have and by your personal preference.

Drench:

Milk   Salt, to taste
Red pepper, to taste   Wine

Dredge:

Cracker crumbs, rolled out as fine   Cayenne pepper
   as possible, or   Salt
Corn flour   Peanut oil for deep frying

Put salt and red pepper in milk and wine. Drench fish. Roll in cracker crumbs. Deep fry at 350 degrees. When they float, they are done. When using corn flour, be sure to put salt and red pepper in it, not just in the milk.

This is better than good, I garontee!

DEEP-FRIED OYSTERS

2 dozen large oysters   Salt, to taste
2 cups corn flour   Peanut oil for deep frying
Ground cayenne pepper

Drain all juice from oysters. Mix corn flour, pepper, and salt. Have peanut oil at 350–365 degrees. Dredge oysters in corn flour mixture and preferably place in a basket and lower into oil. Cook just a few minutes, depending on size of oysters. When oyster floats and is brown, it is cooked.

Pour out on paper napkin or brown paper to drain. Serve immediately.

Louisiana oysters are the best in the world!

BOILED SHRIMP

Salt, depending on the amount of shrimp you use. You need a lot of salt, almost a brine.
3 large onions, quartered
3 to 4 lemons, cut in half

Red pepper, to taste
2 large cloves of garlic, halved
1 or 2 bags crab boil
Shrimp

Put everything in a large pot of water except the shrimp. Boil at least 30 minutes, cooking the onions and garlic. Then put the shrimp in the pot and bring to a boil. Your cooking time depends on the size of the shrimp, but 3 minutes will usually cook most size shrimp. When shrimp float, they are done. Cut the fire off, and leave them soaking in the juices for about 10 or 15 minutes. Real large shrimp may have to cook longer, but not much. DO NOT OVERCOOK. Cool immediately. Peel and eat.

Be careful when you get the shrimp out of the pot because this is as hot as 12 yards of you-know-where.

DEEP-FRIED SOFT-SHELLED CRAB

Drench:

2 cups white wine
Onion powder, to taste
Louisiana hot sauce (cayenne pepper hot sauce)

Garlic powder, to taste

Dredge:

Corn flour or cracker crumbs
Red pepper
Salt

Run crabs through drench of wine, onion powder, Louisiana hot sauce, and garlic powder. Then roll them in corn flour mixed with salt and red pepper. Deep fry at 350 degrees. When they float, they are done. They should be light brown and crispy.

Before you drench crabs, lift edges and remove the lungs, which are tubular looking, and remove eyes and mouth by cutting them off.

MARINATED FRIED FISH FILLETS

Fish fillets
Louisiana hot sauce (cayenne pepper hot sauce)
Salt
Corn flour
Peanut oil for deep frying

Place fish fillets in a bowl or stainless steel pan big enough to hold the fillets you wish to fry. Put Louisiana hot sauce over fish—so that when you stir the fish real well, each piece of fish is coated with hot sauce. Marinate for at least 3 or 4 hours, overnight if you wish (refrigerate).

Salt corn flour to taste. Put enough peanut oil in deep fry pot so that fillets can be deep-fried at 350–365 degrees. Fry until brown—just a few minutes.

You may think that these will be HOT, but they are not!

CRAWFISH MAQUE-CHOU

½ cup bacon drippings or cooking oil
1 cup chopped onion
½ cup chopped bell pepper
1 cup chopped parsley
1 TBS finely chopped garlic
2 to 3 cups whole grain corn, fresh or canned
1 cup dry white wine
1 to 2 cups water
1 TBS. Louisiana hot sauce or ground cayenne pepper
Salt, to taste
1 TBS. Worcestershire sauce
2 lbs. crawfish tails

Sauté onions and bell pepper in oil until clear. Add parsley and garlic. Add corn, stir. Add wine, water, and seasonings, stir. Cook on a simmer, covered, for about 30 minutes. Add crawfish tails and simmer for about 1 hour longer.

Maque-chou is always made with corn. Some peoples add other t'ings.

CRAWFISH PIE

4 TBS. flour (for roux)
¼ cup cooking oil (for roux)
2 TBS. olive oil or cooking oil
   (for roux)
½ cup chopped onion
½ cup chopped fresh mushrooms
½ cup chopped green onions
½ to 1 cup water
1 tsp. chopped garlic

½ cup English peas, cooked and
   drained
½ cup diced carrots, cooked until
   tender
Salt, to taste
Louisiana hot sauce or ground
   red pepper, to taste
1 lb. crawfish meat

Make a roux (see my recipe). Add onions, mushrooms, green onions, and garlic. Stir. Add water. Bring to a boil. Add peas, carrots, salt, and Louisiana hot sauce. Turn heat off and add crawfish. Mix well.

While this is being done, either make pie crust (see my recipe) or use a frozen pie crust.

Put all of the ingredients in a pie pan with the pie crust and top it with another pie crust. Punch holes to let any steam out.

Bake in oven at 325 degrees for 1 hour until crust is golden brown.

OYSTER ROCKEFELLA CASSEROLE

1 medium onion, chopped fine
3 TBS. finely chopped parsley
2 TBS. finely chopped celery
¼ cup olive oil
1 10 oz. package frozen spinach,
   thawed and drained

1 tsp. salt
2 TBS. Louisiana hot sauce
   (cayenne pepper hot sauce)
1 cup seasoned bread crumbs
18 medium oysters and juice

Cook onions, parsley, and celery in olive oil until tender. Add spinach, salt, and Louisiana hot sauce. Cook for about 5 minutes, then add ½ cup bread crumbs. Stir all together, then place on the bottom of a greased casserole. Place oysters over spinach mixture; pour juice over top. Sprinkle rest of bread crumbs over oysters. Bake in 400-degree oven about 20 minutes.

Serves 4 to 6.

Meats

Liver in Mustard Sauce
Deep-Fried Chicken
Deep-Fried Turkey
Baked Tongue
Barbecue Goat
Boston Butt and Cabbage
Embrochette Beef and Shrimp
Chicken I-Wonder-What
Smoked Beef Roast and Pork Roast
Au Justin Gravy
Stuffed Beef and Pork Roasts
Beef Steaks on Barbecue Pit
Chicken Sauce Piquant
Louisiana Smoked Ham
Louisiana Smoked Sausage
Broiled Lamb Chops with Mushrooms
Baked Corned Beef Hash
Smoked Barbecued Pork Ribs
Pasta and Louisiana Smoked Sausage
Pickled Beef Tongue
Mock Chicken Salad
Tasso Omelet
Mustard Chicken
Italian Sausage Spaghetti Sauce

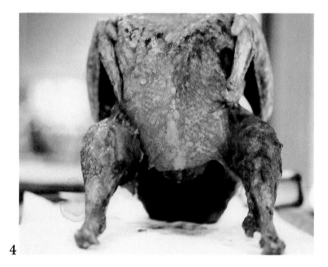

LIVER IN MUSTARD SAUCE

Salt
Ground red cayenne pepper
4 slices liver, ½- to ¾-inch thick
Oleo

1 cup chopped shallots
1 cup dry white wine
1 TBS. creole or poupon mustard

Salt and pepper liver. Sauté liver over medium to high heat in the oleo. Remove liver and keep warm. Pour off some of melted oleo. In what is left, sauté shallots until clear or tender. Add white wine. Bring to boil. Add mustard and blend into mixture. Stir and simmer for a few minutes.

Put liver on platter and pour sauce over it.

DEEP-FRIED CHICKEN

Chicken halves
Salt

Ground red cayenne pepper
Peanut oil

Dry the chicken. Sprinkle with salt and cayenne pepper. Deep fry at 350 degrees until brown. Chicken will float when done.

This chicken is usually served with dirty rice or with barbecue sauce.

DEEP-FRIED TURKEY

1 turkey
Salt

Ground cayenne pepper
Peanut oil, enough to cover

Turkey should be clean and dry, inside and out. Using shaker, cover carcass inside and out with salt. Shake on cayenne pepper in same manner. Peanut oil should be in a large pot and heated to 325–350 degrees. Pot should be large enough for turkey to fit and oil must cover bird completely. Be careful that the pot is large enough that the oil doesn't overflow. Put bird in the pot slowly, being careful not to splash hot oil. Fry about 4 minutes to the pound. Small birds cook more quickly, large birds take longer. Test for doneness at the thigh joint.

Once you eat this turkey, your oven will get cobwebs at Thanksgiving. This turkey doesn't get dry like most cooked turkeys do.

BAKED TONGUE

1 beef tongue
Salt
Red pepper

Boil tongue in seasoned water until it is tender when punctured with a fork, 45 minutes to 1 hour. Remove from water and cool (do not let it get too cold). Peel outer layer of tough skin from tongue. Slice tongue ½ inch thick, not quite through.

Place in a baking pan and pour sauce over the tongue.

Sauce:

1 medium onion, minced
½ cup finely chopped parsley
1 tsp. minced garlic
3½ cups tomato sauce or fresh
    tomatoes, skinned

½ cup red or dry white wine
Salt, to taste
Red pepper, to taste

In a skillet, sauté minced onion and parsley until tender. Add garlic. Stir, and sauté until tender. Add tomato sauce, bring to simmer. Add wine, salt, and pepper, mixing well. When mixture is hot and flavors are well blended, pour over tongue. Put in 350-degree oven for 20 to 30 minutes.

Serve sliced tongue with sauce poured over top. Goes great with rice.

BARBECUE GOAT

1 dressed goat—undressed I
    mean—cut up in pieces that
    will fit on the grill

Salt
Red cayenne pepper
Bacon drippings

Marinate meat overnight in goat marinade (see my recipe). Put goat on medium-hot grill. After the meat has warmed up a little, spread bacon drippings over meat with your hands. Return to heat and cook slowly, basting frequently until done. This takes several hours. You can also rub bacon drippings over once more if goat meat isn't too hot.

BOSTON BUTT AND CABBAGE

Salt, to taste
Ground cayenne pepper
1 Boston butt
1 small head of cabbage, shredded

1 large onion, sliced thin
2 cups chablis wine
3 TBS. Lea & Perrins
  Worcestershire sauce

Salt and pepper Boston butt. Place butt in a roaster, then put the shredded cabbage and onions around it. Mix wine and Lea & Perrins real well; you may want to add about 1 tsp. salt for vegetables. Pour liquid over cabbage—NOT OVER BOSTON BUTT. Cover and bake in 325-degree oven for 2½ to 3 hours or until meat is done.

EMBROCHETTE BEEF AND SHRIMP

Beef, cut in 1-inch pieces
Mushrooms
Shrimp

Stuffed olives
Onions, in large pieces
Bell pepper, in large pieces

Thread all ingredients onto skewer and grill until done. Baste with a basting sauce. These do not take long to cook.

CHICKEN I-WONDER-WHAT

Salt
Red pepper
2 large fryers, cut up
Lime slices

1 cup Falernum
1 cup chablis wine
Lime juice

Salt and pepper chicken. Place in baking pan with lime slices on each piece of chicken. Mix falernum, wine, and lime juice. Pour down side of pan (not on chicken). Cover with aluminum foil, and tuck foil around pan. Bake in 325-degree oven, basting occasionally until chicken is cooked, about 1 hour.

This can be done on a barbecue pit with ease. Just watch chicken as you baste it.

Basting a brisket.

SMOKED BEEF ROAST AND PORK ROAST

1 20-lb. beef roast
1 15-lb. pork roast
10 to 20 cloves garlic, whole

10 to 20 cayenne peppers, fresh
    from the garden or pickled
10 green onions, whole

Prepare the smoker cooker with the following seasonings in water pan and then follow the manufacturer's instructions:

1 cup red or dry white wine
1 whole onion
1 or 2 cloves garlic, whole
1 TBS. liquid smoke
1 tsp. dried mint

2 TBS. parsley
6 drops Peychaud's bitters or 3
    drops Angostura bitters
2 TBS. Worcestershire sauce
Water

Stick a knife into each roast in several places, making a deep puncture. With fingers, push 1 clove garlic in each hole, then a long pepper and a green onion. Slice the pepper and onion off even with the surface of the meat. Sprinkle the roasts with salt and red pepper. When you get your fire going and are ready to put the meat on the smoker cooker, place some pre-soaked smoking wood (such as pecan or hickory) on the briquets. Place seasonings in water pan, then add water all the way to the top of the pan. Place beef roast, then pork roast, in cooker and let them cook. I usually put these on at about 11 P.M. and let them cook while I sleep. One 10-lb. bag of charcoal will usually do.

AU JUSTIN GRAVY

½ cup flour (for roux)
¼ cup oil (for roux)

Cold water
Juice from smoker cooker

After making a small roux (see my recipe), add enough cold water to blend roux. Then add as much juice from smoker cooker pan as you wish. It has all the juice and the tasty fat from the meat that was cooked. Simmer, stirring frequently, until gravy thickens slightly. Serve over rice.

STUFFED BEEF AND PORK ROASTS

1 20-lb. beef roast, chuck or round
1 15-lb. pork roast, loin, or ham,
   or 2 Boston butts

Stuff Each Roast with:

Garlic
Green onion

Fresh cayenne peppers (pickled
   ones can be used)

Rub with:

Salt
Ground cayenne pepper

By "stuff" I mean poke a hole with a slender knife in the meat. Then push in garlic, onion, and peppers. Rub meat with salt and ground cayenne pepper. Wash your hands!

Place on barbecue pit, turning frequently and basting. The pork usually takes longer to cook.

BEEF STEAKS ON BARBECUE PIT

If your barbecue pit does not have a separate fire box, keep your fire on one end and place wet pecan, hickory, or whatever wood you use to smoke. Then place steaks on other end, basting with basting sauce. To tell how they are cooking (rare, medium, etc.) gently press a fork on top. If meat is still soft, it's rare. As the steak cooks, it gets firmer. Turn steaks frequently after they are seared on both sides, basting each time.

CHICKEN SAUCE PIQUANT

2 cups bacon drippings (for roux)
6 cups plain flour (for roux)
7 cups chopped onion
1 cup chopped bell pepper
3 cups chopped green onions
1 cup chopped celery
3 cups chopped parsley
¼ cup chopped garlic
Bacon drippings to brown off
    chicken
20 lbs. chicken (baking hens), cut
    up in 2-inch-long pieces

Water
1 lb. mushrooms, sliced
16 cups tomato sauce
8 cups chablis wine
1½ pints olives, stuffed with
    pimentos
6 TBS. Lea & Perrins
    Worcestershire sauce
8 TBS. Louisiana hot sauce or 2
    tsp. ground cayenne pepper
1 tsp. dried mint, crushed
6 TBS. salt

Make a roux (see my recipe). Add onions, bell pepper, green onions, and celery and sauté until onions are tender and clear. Add parsley and garlic and sauté.

Brown off chicken while roux is being made. After onions, etc. are tender, add water to bring roux to a smooth paste. Add all other ingredients and enough water to cover well. Bring to a boil, and then cut heat. Cook for about 4 to 6 hours.

Serve over spaghetti. This is for a party and will serve 20 to 40 people. You can freeze what you don't eat.

LOUISIANA SMOKED HAM

1 fully cooked ham
1 cup creole-style mustard

1 cup honey (or more, depending
    on the size of the ham)

Line a large baking pan with foil, leaving plenty of foil to make a tent. Put ham on foil. Cover the ham with creole mustard. Pour honey over mustard. Make a tent over ham with foil. Place ham in large baking pan and put on covered section of barbecue pit. Cook for about 1 hour or maybe 1½ hours, until it's heated through.

Joe Gautreau, the world champion jambalaya cook, and a couple of his singing cookers, or cooking singers.

LOUISIANA SMOKED SAUSAGE

Some hot and some mild sausage
in casings

Cooking oil for deep fat frying
Barbecue grill

Cut sausage in 2- to 3-inch lengths, then slice lengthwise. Have cooking oil at 350–365 degrees. Place sausage in wire basket, and lower into oil for about 3 to 5 minutes or less. Take out and drain. 'Twill be nice and crisp. Or you can put the sausage on the grill and heat through. It's already fully cooked.

When we say some hot and some mild, we make sausage both ways. You can deep fry either or both at the same time.

BROILED LAMB CHOPS
WITH MUSHROOMS

1½ sticks oleo or butter
1 cup dry white wine (chablis or
sauterne)
3 TBS. liquid mint sauce (or 3
tsp. dried mint)
1 tsp. Louisiana hot sauce or ½
tsp. ground red pepper

1 tsp. salt
1 lb. fresh mushrooms
1 TBS. dried parsley
1 tsp. dried mint
1 pat (1 tsp.) butter or oleo on
each chop
8 lamb chops

Make a sauce in a frying pan, using all the ingredients except the chops and the pats of butter or oleo. Cook on medium heat then low heat until mushrooms are tender. Put chops in a greased pan and put pats of butter or oleo on each. Broil to taste (they are best when cooked about medium).

To serve, place chops on dinner plate and serve sauce of mushrooms and mint on them.

BAKED CORNED BEEF HASH

½ cup chopped onion
2 TBS. chopped bell pepper
1 TBS. olive oil
1 TBS. bacon drippings or
   cooking oil
2 TBS. dried parsley
1 tsp. chopped garlic

1 lb. canned corned beef
1 cup diced, half-cooked potatoes
2 tsp. Louisiana hot sauce or ¼
   tsp. ground cayenne pepper
Salt
1 TBS. Lea & Perrins
   Worcestershire sauce

Sauté onions and pepper in mixture of olive oil and bacon drippings and cook until they are tender. Add parsley and garlic. Add corned beef and cook a little while to blend all ingredients together. Add potatoes, hot sauce, salt, and Lea & Perrins. Blend all together. Put in baking dish and bake at 325 degrees for 20 minutes.

Serves 4 to 6.

SMOKED BARBECUED PORK RIBS

Salt
Red cayenne pepper
Pork ribs

Dried mint
Pan of water under grill

Salt and pepper ribs and sprinkle with dried mint. Start fire in fire box. When flame has gone down, put pecan or hickory wood on coals (first soak wood in water for a while). Place ribs on grill. Do not let fire get too hot. If your barbecue pit does not have a separate fire box, place the fire on one end away from ribs.

Baste with basting sauce. Serve with barbecue sauce spread on the ribs.

Little men fight big men to get to eat dese ribs and win, I garontee.

PASTA AND
LOUISIANA SMOKED SAUSAGE

½ cup chopped bell pepper
½ cup olive oil
2 cups chopped green onions
1 cup chopped parsley
½ cup chopped celery
½ tsp. dried mint
1 **TBS. Louisiana hot sauce** or ½
  tsp. ground cayenne pepper

3 8 oz. cans tomato sauce
2 cups chablis wine
1 lb. smoked sausage, sliced
  ½-inch thick
Salt, to taste
1 lb. pasta

Sauté bell pepper in half of the olive oil until tender. Add green onions and parsley and cook until onions are tender. Add celery, mint, Louisiana hot sauce, tomato sauce, and wine. Bring to a boil. Add sausage and lower heat to a simmer. Add salt. Cook for about 1 hour. Serve over pasta.

Cook pasta in salted water with the other half of the olive oil. Bring water to a rolling boil. Put pasta (spaghetti) in water and cook until tender. I fling mine against the wall; if it sticks, it's done.

PICKLED BEEF TONGUE

Beef tongue
Salt
Enough water to cover
Red cayenne pepper

Garlic, chopped fine
Dried mint
Cider vinegar

Salt water in a pot to cover tongue. Bring water to boil. Put tongue in and cook until tender, about 1½ hours. Let cool in the water. Take tongue out, and peel outer skin.

Slice tongue ½ inch thick. Salt and red pepper each slice. Lower slices into a jar, putting a little garlic and dried mint between each slice. Pour enough vinegar to cover well over tongue. Close jar and put in refrigerator for at least 24 hours.

My friend Maurice Dantin is a big help making a jambalaya. This one is not quite did, but almost. We had a feast that day, I garontee.

MOCK CHICKEN SALAD

1 large cooked beef tongue,
  ground extra course or cut up
  fine
½ cup finely chopped green olives
1 cup finely chopped onions
1½ cups chopped dill pickles

Mayonnaise
1 TBS. Louisiana hot sauce or
  ground cayenne pepper, to taste
Salt, to taste
2 TBS. Lea & Perrins
  Worcestershire sauce

Mix all ingredients real well using as much mayonnaise as you like to keep the salad from being too dry.

TASSO OMELET

3 eggs per person
Milk (optional)
Peanut oil or shortening for
  frying

Tasso, thinly sliced

Break eggs in a bowl. Use a fork or a whisk to beat eggs until frothy. The milk should be beaten with eggs if you are using it. Pour the eggs into your greased omelet cooking pan and make an omelet in the usual way. When the eggs are almost to where you like them, place the tasso over half of the eggs. Flip the other half over. If you want to cook the eggs a little bit more, cover for about 1 minute. Serve immediately. The tasso is so well seasoned that no salt or red pepper is needed.

MUSTARD CHICKEN

Salt
Red cayenne pepper
2 fryer chickens, cut up
½ cup peanut or cooking oil
1 cup chopped parsley
2 cups dry white wine (chablis)

8 oz. (1 cup) poupon mustard
2 TBS. soy sauce
2 tsp. onion powder
1 tsp. garlic powder
4 hard-boiled eggs, grated fine

Salt and pepper chicken. Then brown off chicken in oil. Remove chicken. Sauté parsley in juice until tender or done. Add wine, mustard, soy sauce, onion powder, and garlic powder, stirring frequently. Cook until smooth. Add grated eggs and cook for about 30 minutes. Pour sauce over chicken and bake in 350-degree oven for 1 to 1½ hours, basting frequently.
Serve over rice. Serves 8.

ITALIAN SAUSAGE SPAGHETTI SAUCE

2 lbs. Italian sausage (link), cut
   into 2-inch lengths
½ cup olive oil
1 cup plain flour
2 cups finely chopped onions
1 cup finely chopped celery
½ cup finely chopped bell pepper
2 cups water
2 cups dry white wine

1 cup dried parsley
1 TBS. finely chopped garlic
1 tsp. red cayenne pepper
3 TBS. Lea & Perrins
   Worcestershire sauce
¼ tsp. dried mint
3 cups tomato sauce
Salt, to taste

Brown sausage off in olive oil (about half cook it), remove from pan and put aside. Add flour to oil that was used and make roux (see my recipe). Add onions, celery, and bell pepper. Stir and cook until tender or clear. Add water and stir until smooth. Add wine, parsley, and garlic. Pour in red pepper, Lea & Perrins, dried mint, and tomato sauce. Stir real well. Bring to a bubbly boil and add salt, to taste. Add sausage. Bring back to a boil. Turn heat down to simmer. Cook for about 3 or 4 hours.
Serve over spaghetti topped with cheese. Should serve 8.

Game

Turtle Sauce Piquant
Wild Duck and Andouille Sauce Piquant
Roast Duck with Apples
Venison Sausage
Turtle Stew
Deep-Fried Dove Bosom (Breast)
Barbecue Rabbit
Rabbit Stew

Here is some turtle sauce piquant.

TURTLE SAUCE PIQUANT

4 cups plain flour (for roux)
2 cups bacon drippings (for roux)
6 cups chopped onion
1 cup chopped bell pepper
½ cup chopped celery
2 cups chopped parsley
2 TBS. chopped garlic
6 cups water
6 lbs. turtle meat
1 cup olive oil, to brown turtle
5 TBS. Louisiana hot sauce or 2
  TBS. ground cayenne pepper

8 cups tomato sauce
4 cups chablis wine
1 can Ro-tel or seasoned canned
  tomatoes, mashed
1 tsp. dried mint
Juice of one lemon
3 TBS. Lea & Perrins
  Worcestershire sauce
Salt, to taste

Make a roux (see my recipe). Add onions and pepper and cook until tender. Add celery and parsley. Cook and stir. Add garlic. Add cold water to roux and stir. While this is being done, brown off turtle meat in olive oil. Put turtle meat in a pot large enough to hold all the ingredients. Add the roux and the rest of the ingredients, mixing well. Cover and bring to a boil. Lower heat and let simmer for 6 hours. More water may be needed. Also adjust salt and cayenne to your taste.

Serve over spaghetti or rice. Serves about 30 people.

WILD DUCK AND
ANDOUILLE SAUCE PIQUANT

1 cup olive oil (for roux)
3 cups plain flour (for roux)
3 cups chopped onion
1 cup chopped bell pepper
3 cups chopped green onions
2 cups chopped parsley
Water
2 TBS. finely chopped garlic
3 cups chablis wine

½ tsp. dried mint, crushed
11 cups tomato sauce
3 TBS. Lea & Perrins
　　Worcestershire sauce
6 tsp. Louisiana hot sauce or 1
　　TBS. ground cayenne pepper
5 tsp. salt
1 lb. andouille, sliced ¼-inch thick
2½ lbs. wild duck breasts

Brown off duck breasts in some olive oil.

Make a roux with oil and flour (see my recipe). Add onions, bell pepper, green onions, and parsley to roux. Stir and cook. Add one cup water and garlic. Cook. Add wine and some more water. Add other seasonings and tomato sauce. Mix well. Add andouille and duck breasts. Stir. Simmer on low heat for 3 to 4 hours. Stir occasionally. Add more salt and cayenne to your taste.

Makes about 3 gallons, so this is for a lot of people. Serve over spaghetti or rice.

ROAST DUCK WITH APPLES

4 or 3 wild ducks (large ducks like
   mallards)
Salt, to taste
Red ground cayenne pepper, to
   taste
6 large apples, quartered, with
   seeds removed

2 cups finely chopped onion
1 TBS. finely chopped garlic
1 cup finely chopped parsley
2 cups red or dry white wine

Cut ducks down the back and clean real well. I reckon all the feathers have already been removed. Salt and pepper duck and place in a large roaster that can be covered. Add the rest of the ingredients with additional salt and pepper. Preheat oven to 325 degrees. Place covered roaster in oven and bake for 2 hours.

Serves 8 or 6 people.

VENISON SAUSAGE

Equal quantities of venison and
   pork (butts, with some fat)
Ground cayenne pepper, to taste

Salt, to taste
Dried mint, small amount,
   crushed fine

Clean all fat and membrane from venison. Cut up into pieces to go in grinder. Cut up pork—it must have some fat or sausage will be dry. In grinder, grind venison and pork, trying to mix them as you go along. This should be ground fine. Season with pepper, salt, and small amount of mint. Then grind again. After mixing real well fry a patty or two for taste. If more seasoning is needed, carefully add it.

This sausage can be made into patties and frozen or put into natural pork casings and either frozen or smoked.

Buddy Gregoire and a snapping turtle. He may have caught dat turtle, but I'm gonna eat it.

TURTLE STEW

1 cup flour (for roux)
¼ cup cooking oil or olive oil (for roux)
¼ cup bacon drippings (for roux)
2 cups chopped onion
½ cup chopped bell pepper
1 cup finely chopped parsley
1 TBS. finely chopped garlic
4 cups water
1 cup dry white wine
1 TBS. lemon juice
2 TBS. Lea & Perrins Worcestershire sauce
Salt
Ground cayenne pepper
4 or 3 lbs. of boned turtle meat

Make a dark roux (see my recipe). Add onions and bell pepper. Cook until tender. Add parsley and garlic. Cook for a few minutes. Add cold water and stir until the mixture is smooth. Add wine, lemon juice, and Worcestershire sauce.

While roux is cooking, salt and pepper turtle meat and brown off in cooking oil. Add to the roux and cook over low fire for about 2 hours. Additional salt and pepper may be needed. If the stew is too thick, add water.

Serve over rice or pasta. Should serve 8 or 10.

DEEP-FRIED DOVE BOSOM (BREAST)

Salt
Red pepper
3 cups plain flour (may take more)
½ tsp. garlic powder
1 tsp. onion powder
12 or 10 dressed dove bosoms (breasts)
Cooking oil (peanut oil preferably), for deep frying

Heat oil to about 350–365 degrees.

Salt and pepper dove bosoms. In a pan deep enough, put flour, garlic powder, onion powder, and a little more salt and pepper. Dredge dove real well and cook in hot oil until golden brown. They should float after a few minutes.

Serves about 6 or 5 people if you have other food.

BARBECUE RABBIT

2 large fryer rabbits
All-Purpose Marinade (see my
   recipe)

Wood for smoking
Charcoal
Barbecue pit

Cut rabbits as if you were going to fry. Marinate in All-Purpose Marinade (see my recipe) for about 1 hour.

While this is being done, get your fire going and soak wood for smoking in water. When your coals are ready (not too hot, about medium) put soaked wood on coals.

Take rabbits from marinade and put on pit. Baste frequently with marinade, turning them each time you baste. This rabbit will turn a nice brown and should not take too long.

Serve with barbecue sauce (see my recipe), which is put on after rabbit is cooked.

RABBIT STEW

1 cup plain flour (for roux)
½ cup cooking oil or bacon
   drippings (for roux)
3 rabbits, cut up
2 cups chopped onion
½ cup chopped bell pepper
½ cup chopped celery
1 cup chopped green onions
½ cup chopped parsley

1 TBS. chopped garlic
3 cups water
2 TBS. Lea & Perrins
   Worcestershire sauce
1 cup dry white wine
Salt, to taste
Ground red cayenne pepper or
   Louisiana hot sauce, to taste

First, cut rabbit up in pieces a little smaller than for frying. Brown this off in cooking oil or bacon drippings and set aside.

Add flour to the oil that is left. You may have to add 1 TBS. of oil or drippings. Stir and make dark brown roux (see my recipe). When roux is brown enough, add onions, bell pepper, and celery. Cook until clear or tender. Add green onions, parsley, and garlic. Cook for a few minutes. Add cold water and stir until mixture is smooth. Add Lea & Perrins, wine, salt, pepper, and then rabbit. Cover. Bring to a boil and cut fire to simmer. Cook for 2 hours, more if you have time. You may need to add more water. Makes about 2 gallons.

La Boucherie

What is a Boucherie?
Salt Pork
Pickled Pork
Hogshead Cheese
Cracklin's
White Pork Boudin
Pig in Cajun Microwave
Grillades
Pork Paté
Fresh Pork Sausage
Boudin Rouge

Hams and sausage are some of the t'ings dat we make at a boucherie.

WHAT IS A BOUCHERIE?

When the weather gets cool, it comes the time to butcher hogs. The neighbors get together to help each other. Water is heated in a vessel big enough to submerge at least half of the largest hog that you plan to kill. The water should be heated to about 165 degrees. If the water is too hot, it will "set" the hair and make it difficult to scrape off. The hog is usually shot in the head with a .22 caliber rifle, then the throat is cut by one stick in the right place to bleed the hog. This blood is caught if Boudin Rouge (red) is made.

Then the hog is placed for a few moments in the hot water and put on a table of some kind. Using dull knives, the hair is scraped off. Sometimes we put a burlap sack in the hot water and rub most of the hair off.

The hog, after scraping, is hung up on a jolly stick that is inserted under the tendons of the rear feet. Then, with a sharp knife, we cut down the belly, being sure not to cut too deep into the intestines. We remove everything—small and large intestines, heart, liver, pancreas, and tongue. The intestines are thoroughly cleaned—and I mean thoroughly. Some are used for casings, and the largest are used for chitterlings. The liver is cooked that day. Some of us pickle the heart and tongue after boiling, or some of us use the heart and tongue in our smoked sausage.

The hog is then cut up country style to make backbone (country style) chops, roasts, butts, hams, and bacon. The belly part is usually fat, and we trim that and cut it up to make cracklin's and grillades. Grillades are lean strips that we cook while working. Cracklin's are the pieces of fat and skin that are fried to make the lard that we use to cook so many things. Then the large pieces are cut, such as the hams. All the scraps are used to make hogshead cheese or sausages. The fresh cuts of meat are refrigerated and some cooked for all the workers. Then sausage-making and smoking will be done.

SALT PORK

Pork shoulder 25 lbs., cut in workable pieces (about 5 or 6 pieces)

Mix 3 lbs. of pickling salt and ½ lb. brown sugar real well. Use about half of the mixture to rub well on all of the meat—massage it into all the cracks and crevices, leaving a thin coating on meat.

Place in a clean crock, and cover with a clean cloth or loose-fitting lid. Cure in a cold place, about 38 degrees Fahrenheit. In about a week, remove meat and coat it again with remaining cure mixture. Cure at least 30 days. Be sure and leave the meat in the container even if you can't see salt.

If you desire, you may smoke the pork.

PICKLED PORK

In a large crock or keg, using pickling salt, make a brine that will float a fresh chicken egg. Add 1 TBS. saltpeter (potassium nitrate) (optional). Place pieces of pork in a container so they are well covered with brine. Cover with a board or plate with a clean brick or stone on it to hold it down. Store in a cool place, preferably in a cooler or refrigerator.

Remove meat in about 6 or 7 days. Stir brine. Put meat back into container. Be sure all meat is covered and kept down by a plate or board with weights on it. Repeat this again in about 6 or 7 days.

Curing time is 30 days. Remove the meat and keep it well refrigerated. If you have a great deal of meat, freeze what you don't use in two weeks' time.

HOGSHEAD CHEESE

——— ◆ ———

1 hog's head, cut into pieces
   (remove eyes and brush teeth)
4 lbs. of pork butt, cut into pieces
4 hog's feet, cleaned real well
4 cups chopped onion
1 cup chopped bell pepper

3 TBS. minced garlic
2 cups chopped parsley
2 cups chopped green onion tops
Salt, black pepper, and cayenne
   pepper, to taste

Put head, pork butt, feet, onions, bell pepper, and garlic in a large pot. Cover with water and boil about 3 hours or until tender. Remove hog's head, pork butt, and feet. Save the stock. Cool the meat, then remove the bones. Grind everything else in a food processor or grinder. To this meat add enough of the stock or juice to soften it up. Add parsley, onion tops, salt, black pepper, and cayenne pepper. Pour into large glass baking dishes and refrigerate overnight—mixture will gel.

To serve, unmold from baking dish and slice; serve with crackers or french bread.

CRACKLIN'S

——— ◆ ———

1 quart of hog lard or water
10 lbs. pork fat with skin, cut into
   1-inch pieces

Salt, to taste

Heat hog lard in a large, heavy pot. If you don't have lard, use water instead. Add pork fat pieces, stirring often to prevent sticking. When they pop or crack they should start to float in oil and get brown. Remove with a slotted spoon and drain on paper towels. While still hot, add salt to taste.

These are better served fresh. But to keep them for a short period of time, seal them in a tightly covered container.

Lard is the grease that is left after making cracklin's. It is poured into jars after it cools and saved for cooking.

An old sausage stuffer dat is still used to make boudin and sausage.

This is what we call a Cajun microwave. You notice dat the fire is on top. I suppose dat some Cajuns went to Hawaii and saw how they do a pig dere. Then dey said dere's got to be a more easier way. So dey came up wit' dis . . . where dey didn't have to dig and undig a hole.

WHITE PORK BOUDIN

3 TBS. bacon drippings
1 cup chopped onion
1 cup chopped fresh parsley
1 TBS. chopped garlic
1 cup water
2 cups cooked rice

4 cups cooked pork, chopped
  (leftovers will work)
Ground cayenne pepper, to taste
1½ tsp. salt, depending on amount
  of salt in leftover pork

Sauté onions in bacon drippings until nearly clear. Add parsley, then garlic. Add water. Cook until the onions are completely cooked. Add rice and blend in real well. Add chopped pork, ground cayenne pepper, and salt if needed.

With sausage stuffer, stuff mixture into natural pork casings. Tie in 4- to 5-inch links. To serve, heat in a pan with a little water until warmed through.

PIG IN CAJUN MICROWAVE

Pig
Green onions
Garlic

Fresh or pickled cayenne pepper
Salt
Red pepper (cayenne)

Stuff the pig with green onions, garlic, and fresh cayenne peppers. By stuffing, I mean poking holes in the pig and putting the garlic, onions, and peppers in these holes. Rub the outside with salt and red pepper. Put in Cajun microwave and cook until done.

A Cajun microwave is a box made from wood, about 18 to 24 inches in depth, with a grill in the bottom to hold meat. The top of this box is thick metal. A fire is built on the top. This top has to be built so that the hot metal does not touch the wood, and also so that it can be removed to check the food. We call it a microwave because compared to cochon du lait (milk-fed pig) which cooks about 18 to 24 hours before an open fire, a Cajun microwave cooks in about 4 to 6 hours.

GRILLADES

To make cracklin's or gratons, you should remove the thin strips of lean meat from the belly part of the hog. Grillades are made from this meat. Put these thin strips in a greased skillet and brown slowly. Add salt and cayenne pepper to taste. You can put these on a barbecue pit. Add salt and pepper, and eat.

PORK PATÉ

1 lb. pork liver, cut into ¼-inch-thick slices
1 onion, chopped
2 TBS. oil
2 lbs. pork loin, cut into chunks
½ tsp. dried mint, crushed fine
1 TBS. salt
1½ tsp. ground cayenne pepper
3 lbs. pork fat
2 bay leaves

Brown liver and onions in oil until liver is whitish and no blood shows. Grind liver, onions, and pork loin in a food processor or food grinder; add the drippings from the pan in which the liver was cooked, the dried mint, salt, and cayenne pepper, and mix well. Cut 1 lb. of the pork fat into ½-inch cubes and boil in the water with the bay leaves for 3 minutes; drain and cool. Mix pork fat with pork meat thoroughly, using your hands and blending fat into the meat and liver. Cut the remaining pork fat into thin strips about 2 inches wide; line the bottom and sides of a heavy baking dish or loaf pan with these strips. Place the pork meat mixture into baking dish and cover top with more slices of fat, making sure the paté is well covered with fat; place bay leaves on top and cover the baking dish with a lid or heavy foil. Bake at 350 degrees for 1 hour and 15 minutes. The fat should be well browned; if it is not, remove cover and bake uncovered until brown. Cool at least 5 to 6 hours before removing from baking dish; keep fat on paté until it is to be served, then remove the fat.

This will keep for about 2 weeks with the fat layers on it. Serve with crackers or on open-face sandwiches.

FRESH PORK SAUSAGE

Using mostly lean pork, with enough fat for flavor, finely grind pork in a meat grinder. Add salt, ground cayenne pepper, and either sage or dried mint. All of this is to taste. By all means use your imagination and common sense, remembering that you can always add seasoning. Mix this real well and run through the grinder again.

You can stuff this in a casing and cook it fresh or you can smoke it. I always fry a patty or two to check my seasoning (and to keep from getting hungry). I love fresh pork sausage made at a boucherie.

BOUDIN ROUGE

1 pint blood from slaughtered   1 TBS. minced garlic
   hog   Salt
1 cup minced onion   Red cayenne pepper
1 cup hog fat   Natural pork casings

When you butcher the hog, be careful about cleanliness. Stick the pig and collect the blood. Fry the minced onions with a small piece of hog fat in a skillet. Add the garlic and sauté slightly. Grind the rest of the hog fat fine and mix it with the blood. Add the onions and garlic. Add salt and cayenne pepper to taste and other seasonings, if used. If you like you may add allspice, nutmeg, or other herbs for a little more flavor. Mix all the ingredients well. Clean the casings well and check for holes. Tie a knot in one end. Pour blood mixture into casing and tie a knot every foot. After you have filled the casing with the blood, go back and knot every 4 inches between the big links as you go. Wash the outside very well and put in a pot of warm water. Cook in the water, but do not let the water boil. The blood is set when the casing is pricked and the blood doesn't run out.

Now you can refrigerate or smoke this boudin rouge.

Vegetables

New Year's Cabbage Rolls
Cabbage and Onions with Louisiana Smoked Sausage
Cabbage and Turnips
Hot Slaw with Tasso
Barbecued Red Beans
Deep-Fried Squash
Boiled Corn
Dirty Rice
Spaghetti
Mustard Greens with Louisiana Smoked Sausage
Deep-Fried Okra
Corn in Foil
Grilled Potatoes
Rice
Baked Yams or Sweet Potatoes
Squash Maurice
Stuffed Potatoes au Wayne
Boiled Burr Artichokes
Succatasso
Soul Food Succatash
Butterbeans with Ham Shanks
Red Bean Casserole
Baked Stuffed Onions with Fresh Pork
Smothered Mirliton

NEW YEAR'S CABBAGE ROLLS

Cabbage leaves, large
Water to blanch or parboil cab-
    bage leaves
2 TBS. bacon drippings
1 cup chopped onion
1 cup chopped parsley
1 TBS. chopped garlic
2 cups ground ham

2 cups cooked black-eyed peas
2 cups cooked rice
Salt, to taste
1 TBS. Louisiana hot sauce or ½
    tsp. ground cayenne pepper
2 eggs, beaten
2 8 oz. cans tomato sauce

Select and clean cabbage leaves. Parboil cabbage leaves so that they are pliable. Sauté in a skillet with bacon drippings, onions, parsley, and garlic. Mix together in a large bowl the ground ham, black-eyed peas, and cooked rice. Add 1 tsp. salt and 1 TBS. Louisiana hot sauce. Add the cooked vegetables to the ham mixture and blend well. Add beaten eggs to the mixture and blend well. Put 1 to 2 TBS. stuffing in each leaf. Roll the leaves around the stuffing and secure with teethpicks if needed. Place stuffed leaves in baking dish and pour tomato sauce over the cabbage rolls, covering them lightly. Bake in oven at 300 degrees for 30 minutes.

Serves 8 people.

Da reason how come dese are call New Year's cabbage rolls is dat in da South, we eat greens for money, pork for happiness, and black-eyed peas for health in da coming year. Also, in South Louisiana, we just got to eat rice.

CABBAGE AND ONIONS WITH LOUISIANA SMOKED SAUSAGE

½ lb. salt meat, cut in 1-inch
   squares
Bacon drippings (enough to
   grease the bottom of your pot)
Water
3 to 2 heads of cabbage, quartered
10 onions, whole
1 large clove garlic, chopped

1 lb. mushrooms
1 cayenne pepper, whole, or 1 tsp.
   ground red cayenne pepper
3 lbs. Louisiana smoked sausage,
   cut in bite-size pieces
2 cups chablis wine
2 tsp. salt, or to taste

Brown the salt meat in bacon drippings. Put in a little water, then add cabbage, onions, garlic, mushrooms, cayenne pepper, and sausage. Add wine. Add enough water to fill the pot halfway. Bring to a boil, then simmer for 2 hours.

Feeds 12 or 10 people.

We put mushrooms in dis dish to raise da social status of da cabbage and to make da onions socially acceptable.

CABBAGE AND TURNIPS

½ to 1 lb. salt pork or pickled pork
1 TBS. olive oil
Water
2 heads cabbage, cut into 6 pieces
   each
6 turnips, peeled and cut in half
6 medium onions, whole

1 small clove of garlic, chopped
2 cups chablis wine
Louisiana hot sauce or cayenne
   pepper, to taste
1 lb. andouille or smoked sausage
Salt, to taste

In a large pot, sauté salt pork or pickled pork in olive oil. Brown slightly, then cover with water. Place cabbage, turnips, onions, and garlic in pot. Add chablis wine and enough water to come up to where you can see it. Add hot sauce or pepper and andouille or smoked sausage. Bring to a boil, then let simmer for 1 to 2 hours. Taste for salt, and add some if necessary.

This is a complete meal for 6 to 12 people, depending on how hungry everyone is.

Tasso is smoked pork. We use it for flavoring other food. But I like it just like this.

HOT SLAW WITH TASSO

2 cups of tasso ham, cubed
Enough bacon drippings to
    brown off tasso and to sauté
    onions and bell pepper
3 cups chopped onions
1 cup chopped bell pepper

3 cans whole tomatoes
1 large cabbage, shredded
Salt, to taste
2 TBS. vinegar
Ground cayenne pepper, to taste

Sauté tasso in bacon drippings. Remove tasso from pan or pot. Put onions and bell pepper in the hot pot and sauté until tender. Add canned whole tomatoes and tasso and bring to a boil. Add cabbage, then salt, vinegar, and cayenne pepper, but taste the mixture first as it may not need the pepper. Bring to a boil and simmer for 2 hours.
Serves 8 to 12 people.

BARBECUED RED BEANS

2 lbs. red kidney beans
1 cup chopped onion
1 TBS. chopped garlic
1 TBS. liquid smoke
1 TBS. Louisiana hot sauce or ¼
    tsp. ground cayenne pepper
1 TBS. Lea & Perrins
    Worcestershire sauce

2 cups dry white wine (chablis or
    sauterne)
8 cups water
2 TBS. parsley flakes (dried
    parsley)
1 TBS. dehydrated sweet pepper

Put all of the above in a bowl and soak or marinate for a few hours or overnight.

2 cups barbecue sauce
½ lb. salt pork or pickled pork
A little grease

Brown off pork in large pot. Add beans and seasoned water mixture. Add barbecue sauce and stir. If necessary, add water to cover well. Bring to a boil and then cut fire back to a slower bubbly boil. Stir occasionally. Cook until tender and then add salt to taste.
Serve over rice if you like. This will serve approximately 10 or 12 people, depending on how hungry they are and whether you have other food.

DEEP-FRIED SQUASH

4-6 yellow squash, cut into ½-inch
  slices

Oil for deep frying
Romano or Parmesan cheese

Drench:

1 cup dry white wine
½ tsp. garlic powder
½ tsp. onion powder

½ tsp. ground cayenne pepper
1 tsp. salt

Dredge:

Corn flour
Salt to taste
Ground cayenne pepper to taste

Mix together all of the ingredients for the drench. Dip squash in this mixture and then in corn flour mixture. Deep fry squash for 1 minute at 350 degrees. Sprinkle with Romano cheese after frying. Serve immediately.

BOILED CORN

Water
Smoked ham hocks
Salt

1 lb. oleo
Salt meat
Corn

Bring water to a boil with all the ingredients except the corn, letting the seasonings cook for about 30 minutes. Put the corn in the pot and cook for about 20 minutes.

How much corn? How long is a piece of string? You should use your judgment on this; however, try these amounts:

Water in a large pot (enough to
  cover the corn real well)
3 or 4 smoked ham hocks
Salt, to taste after tasting water

1 lb. oleo
2 lbs. fat salt pork
2 dozen ears of corn

Dis recipe will serve about 6 to 4 peoples because some of dem are goin' to eat 3 ears, I garontee.

DIRTY RICE

2 lbs. lean ground beef
2 lbs. lean ground pork
1 lb. chicken giblets (ground)
3 TBS. olive oil
2 cups finely chopped onion
2 cups finely chopped green
   onions
¾ cup finely chopped bell (sweet)
   pepper
1 cup finely chopped parsley
1 cup finely chopped celery
¼ cup finely chopped garlic

1 tsp. dried mint, crushed
1 tsp. ground cayenne pepper
2 tsp. Louisiana hot sauce
   (cayenne pepper hot sauce)
3 TBS. Lea & Perrins
   Worcestershire sauce
4 tsp. salt, or to taste
1 cup chablis wine
Water
2 lbs. long grain rice, cooked
   separately (see recipe)

Mix all of the meats in a heavy pot on a medium-hot burner. Add all the other ingredients except rice. Cook on medium heat approximately 4 hours. Stir often. Add cooked rice, mixing thoroughly. Cook over low heat about 30 minutes.

This recipe is for a real party—12 to 30 people if you serve something else to eat.

SPAGHETTI

Water (enough to cover spaghetti
   real well)
2 TBS. olive oil

1 TBS. salt
2 lbs. spaghetti

Boil the water. Add olive oil and salt. Add spaghetti to water. Cook until tender. Pour into colander and serve while hot.

If you have a wall handy, t'row a string of spaghetti up against de wall. If it stick, it's done.

Lunch at my sister Olivette's house wit' some good friends. The food was good, but the company was better.

MUSTARD GREENS WITH LOUISIANA SMOKED SAUSAGE

1 cup Louisiana smoked sausage
   (sliced into ½-inch pieces)
1 **TBS.** bacon drippings
Water (enough to make juice)
¾ cup chopped onion

1 **TBS.** chopped garlic
2 large bunches mustard greens
1 cup white wine
Salt and Louisiana hot sauce, to
   taste (cayenne pepper hot sauce)

Brown sausage slightly in the bacon drippings, then cover with water. Add onions and garlic. Bring to a boil. Place mustard greens in the pot. Add the wine, additional water (if needed), salt, and hot sauce. Bring to a boil, then cook for 1 to 1½ hours on medium heat.

DEEP-FRIED OKRA

4 to 8 cups okra, cut in ½- to
   ¾-inch pieces
Peanut oil for deep frying

Drench:

3 cups milk
2 cups chablis wine
1 **TBS.** Louisiana hot sauce
   (cayenne pepper hot sauce)

1 **TBS.** soy sauce

Mix all of the above real well to be used as a drench.

Dredge:

3 cups corn flour
1 tsp. garlic powder

1 tsp. onion powder
Salt, to taste

In a baking pan, mix corn flour, garlic powder, onion powder, and salt. Drench okra well in liquid mixture. Roll in corn flour mixture. Have oil at about 350–365 degrees. Put some okra in a basket, if possible, and lower into oil. Don't let the oil boil over. When brown and floating, the okra is cooked. Let it drain and put on paper towel or brown paper. Serve immediately.

CORN IN FOIL

Rub corn with oleo. Wrap in foil. Place on grill and cook. This corn wrapped in foil should cook in about 20 or 30 minutes. Using cloth pot lifters or mittens, feel the corn and you can tell by the softness if it is cooked.

Better put a few extra ears on for hungry peoples.

GRILLED POTATOES

Potatoes
Bacon drippings

Rub potatoes with bacon drippings. Wrap in foil and place on grill. After about 20 or 30 minutes, using a pot lifter or mitten, gently squeeze. When the potato is soft, it is done.

You can make a good salad out of the extras the next day.

Always grill a few extra potatoes just in case someone like me is wit' you to eat.

RICE

Rice	**Salt**
Water	**1 TBS. olive oil or margarine**

Put rice in a heavy pot. Add water to cover by 1 inch. Add a little salt to taste. Add olive oil or margarine. Cook over medium heat, stirring occasionally, until all the water is cooked out. Reduce heat to a simmer and cover. Simmer about 45 minutes. Don't raise lid or cover to check until 45 minutes to 1 hour has passed.

BAKED YAMS OR SWEET POTATOES

Bacon drippings
Yams (sweet potatoes) unpeeled

Massage yams well with bacon drippings. Place on baking pan or sheet and put in 350-degree oven for 45 minutes to 1 hour. Using pot lifter, pad, or hot mitten, gently press on yams after 45 minutes to see if they are soft or fully cooked. Serve with butter or margarine, if desired.

If these are cooked on a barbecue pit, wrap them in foil and check frequently until they feel soft.

Serve one yam to a person, so put as many in the oven or on the pit as you may need, with a few extra in case someone is hungry.

SQUASH MAURICE

4 acorn squash
4 slices of bacon
1 onion, chopped
½ tsp. thyme seasoning, coarse
   kind

Salt
Pepper
½ cup (or more) Italian bread
   crumbs
1 cup sour cream

Parboil squash 15 to 20 minutes; let cool. Fry bacon in skillet; set aside bacon and drain all but two tablespoons of bacon drippings from skillet. Sauté onion in bacon drippings until tender. Chop top from squash and remove pulp; save the shells. Remove the seeds. Chop or mash the pulp and sauté it with the tender onions. Add thyme, salt, and pepper. Sauté another 10 to 15 minutes over low heat. Fold the bread crumbs and sour cream into the onion and pulp mixture. Mix well and place in the squash shells. Crumble bacon over squash. Bake in a 375-degree oven for 15 minutes or until heated through and through.

Maurice is a Cajun dat live in Mississippi. But he still don' los' his abilities in the kitchen.

137

We grow a garden every year. Here I am petting the peppers so they will get positive foodback.

STUFFED POTATOES AU WAYNE

6 large potatoes
Chopped green onions
2 tsp. garlic powder
½ lb. butter or oleo
6 TBS. sour cream

2 tsp. black pepper
Cooked shrimp, crab, or crawfish,
   2 TBS. per potato, chopped fine
¼ to ½ tsp. ground cayenne pepper

Rub each potato with cooking oil. Bake potatoes 1 hour. Cut the top off lengthwise and scoop out and reserve the middle. Save the potato shells for stuffing.

Mix the rest of the ingredients together with the reserved cooked potato filling. Fill potato shells with stuffing. Sprinkle with cayenne pepper, if desired. Wrap in foil or Saran Wrap, then heat in microwave, oven, or grill until hot.

This recipe is for six potatoes.

From Irish potato to Idaho potato to Cajun potato—da bes' yet, I garontee.

BOILED BURR ARTICHOKES

4 to 6 fresh young burr artichokes
1 cup olive oil
2 large onions, quartered
½ cup lemon juice
2 large cloves garlic
3 to 4 cups dry white wine

2 TBS. Louisiana hot sauce
   (cayenne pepper hot sauce)
2 TBS. Lea & Perrins
   Worcestershire sauce
Salt, to taste
Water

Wash the artichokes well and let them drain. Put in a pot large enough for liquids to cover them, or nearly so. Pour olive oil over them and put onions, lemon juice, and garlic in pot. Pour wine over artichokes and add Louisiana hot sauce and Worcestershire sauce. Add enough water to float artichokes. Add salt, to taste. Cook, covered, over medium flame, adding water as needed. (It is not necessary to keep the artichokes covered with liquid when they near completion of cooking.) Cook until outside leaves are very tender. After artichokes are done, turn off heat, and keep them covered.

You can eat them hot or cool and serve with seasoned mayonnaise.

SUCCATASSO

1 cup chopped onion
½ cup bell pepper
1 TBS. chopped garlic
½ cup dried parsley
1 cup dry wine
2 cups chopped tasso
4 cups precooked corn, shaved off
   cob

1 TBS. Louisiana hot sauce or 1
   tsp. ground cayenne pepper
1 TBS. Lea & Perrins
   Worcestershire sauce
Salt, to taste
6 cups cubed ripe fresh tomatoes

Put onions, bell pepper, garlic, and parsley in wine in a pot or deep frying pan. Cook for 30 minutes. Add the rest of the ingredients and cook for 2 hours over a low heat.

SOUL FOOD SUCCATASH

½ lb. bacon, cut into small pieces
1 lb. smoked pigtails, cut into 1- to
   2-inch lengths
2 15 oz. cans green lima beans or 4
   cups cooked lima beans

2 cans whole grain corn
1 can Ro-tel (hot canned
   tomatoes)
Salt, to taste

Cook bacon until crisp or completely cooked. Add smoked pigtails and sauté for about 5 minutes. Add lima beans and corn. Then add Ro-tel, after mashing with a fork. Add salt, to taste. Bring to a boil and then simmer with a lid on pot for 45 minutes.

BUTTERBEANS WITH HAM SHANKS

1 lb. ham shanks
6 cups water
1 cup chopped onion
1 TBS. Lea & Perrins
   Worcestershire sauce

2 tsp. Louisiana hot sauce
   (cayenne pepper hot sauce)
2 lbs. butterbeans
2 cups dry white wine
Salt, if needed

Have shanks cut in ¾-inch-wide slices, bone in. Place shanks in pot and cover with water. Add onions, and cook for about 15 minutes. Cook for a few minutes, 5 or 10. Add Lea & Perrins and hot sauce. Add beans, then wine, and some more water. The beans will take up some of the water. If any water is needed, add hot water. Cook until beans are tender.

RED BEAN CASSEROLE

2 cups chopped green onions
2 TBS. olive oil
½ cup parsley
½ cup sweet pepper
1 tsp. chili powder
1 cup tomato sauce
1 cup dry white wine
¼ tsp. dried mint, crushed
1 TBS. chopped garlic

1 cup seasoned bread crumbs
2 cups cooked rice
1 tsp. Louisiana hot sauce
   (cayenne pepper hot sauce)
4 cups cooked (leftover) red beans,
   with juice drained
1 cup of red bean juice
3 cups grated cheddar

Sauté green onions, parsley, and sweet pepper in olive oil. Mix all ingredients except cheddar, and put in casserole. Place cheese on top and bake in a 350-degree oven for 1½ hours.

You see how I'm ignore those smoker cookers? That's how easy
they are to use. You put it together and then stan' back.

BAKED STUFFED ONIONS
WITH FRESH PORK

4 large onions, cut in half
1½ lbs. ground pork
1 cup finely chopped onion
¾ tsp. garlic powder, or to taste
Salt, to taste

Red cayenne pepper, to taste
1 TBS. Lea & Perrins
   Worcestershire sauce
¾ cup dry white wine
½ cup water

After cutting large onions in half as if you were going to make onion rings, hollow the onion out, making 3 or 4 rings. Grease baking pan.

Mix pork with chopped onions, garlic powder, salt, pepper, and Lea & Perrins. Mix well. Stuff meat mixture into onion halves and place in baking pan. Pour wine and water down the side—NOT ON ONIONS. Bake in a 325-degree oven for about 1½ hours.

SMOTHERED MIRLITON

Bacon
Mirliton
Onions, chopped

Garlic, chopped
Red cayenne pepper, to taste
Salt, to taste

Fry off bacon and remove from skillet. Slice mirliton lengthwise and remove seed. After this, cut the mirliton up in thin pieces. Place in cold water. Put chopped onions in with bacon fat. Fry until tender. Add garlic and pepper and cook. Add mirliton and bacon pieces. Cover and stir frequently. When tender, mirliton is ready to eat.

Amounts are by volume: if you have two cups of cut-up mirlitons, then you should have two cups of chopped onions.

Desserts

Strawberry Sherbet
Watermelon Sherbet
Melon Balls in Falernum
Canteloupe Sherbet
Mama's Strawberry Shortcake
Pecan Brittle
Doris's Pralines
Peggy's Benne Seed Brittle
Garden Cake à la Dot
Rhubarb Pie
Fig Cake
Pie Crust
Roasted Pecans
Yeola's Bread Pudding

This is my frien', former Louisiana Governor Jimmie Davis, who wrote everybody's favorite song, "You Are My Sunshine." Also, too, he is a good knife and fork man.

STRAWBERRY SHERBET

1 pint cleaned ripe strawberries,
    blended in a purée
2 eggs, beaten well
¾ cup sugar

Dash of salt
2 tsp. Falernum or ½ tsp. vanilla
    extract
3 cups milk, regular or lowfat

Combine all the ingredients in the cream can of your ice cream maker and mix well. Follow manufacturer's instructions on operating the machine.

WATERMELON SHERBET

2 cups watermelon purée
3 eggs, well beaten
¾ cup sugar

Dash salt
4 cups milk, regular or lowfat

Combine all the ingredients in the cream can of your ice cream maker and mix well. Follow manufacturer's instructions on operating machine.

MELON BALLS IN FALERNUM

Honeydew
Canteloupe

Watermelon
Falernum

Scoop melons with melon-baller and put into bowl. Pour Falernum over them and mix well.

Falernum is a delightfully flavored syrup made in New Orleans.

CANTELOUPE SHERBET

2 cups canteloupe purée
3 eggs, well beaten
¾ cup sugar

Dash salt
Dash cinnamon
4 cups milk, regular or lowfat

Combine all the ingredients in the cream can of your ice cream maker and mix well. Follow manufacturer's instructions on operating machine.

MAMA'S STRAWBERRY SHORTCAKE

First, make a pie crust, ¼ to ½ inch thick (see my recipe). Put half of the crust in the bottom of a baking vessel (pan, Corningware, Pyrex). Put the other half of the crust in another pan, cut in strips. Bake crust until brown. Remove and let cool.

Take 4 to 6 cups of strawberries, stemmed and sprinkled with as much sugar as you like. Let these marinate for 1 hour or so. You can put some cinnamon with them if you like. After the crust has cooled, put strawberries in pan with crust and cover with strips of crust. Put in refrigerator for about 1 hour.

Dis is how Mama made strawberry shortcake. She lived to be 96 year old and was a wondermus cook. Dere was never anyt'ing left on da plate when she cook.

PECAN BRITTLE

4 cups pecans
4 cups sugar
1 cup Pet milk

Pinch salt
1 cup cane syrup
¼ lb. margarine

Roast pecans in heavy skillet on medium heat, stirring constantly until dark brown.

Combine sugar, milk, salt, margarine, and cane syrup in heavy sauce pan and cook to soft-ball stage (240–250 degrees). Add roasted pecans and continue to cook and stir until the mixture thickens. Pour onto a well-greased cookie sheet—one with sides works best. Let cool. Break into pieces to serve.

DORIS'S PRALINES

4 cups sugar
4 TBS. Karo syrup
1 can condensed milk
1 can water

4 to 5 cups pecans
1 TBS. butter or oleo
1 tsp. vanilla

Mix all ingredients except butter, vanilla, and pecans. Cook on low fire until the mixture forms a soft ball in cold water. Remove from fire. Add butter, vanilla, and pecans, and beat until the mixture holds its shape. Spoon onto buttered wax paper. (Add old newspaper under your wax paper.)

If candy gets hard before all is spooned out, add a little water, and heat over. Or you can let it stand on low heat while spooning out.

Doris is the much better half (wife) of my good friend Gordon Martin, the sheriff of St. James Parish. Every Christmas Eve we go by to see them after watching the bonfires that are burned on the levees along the Mississippi River to light the way for Papa Noel (Santa Claus).

Here are my friends Peggy and Lew Woods from Lutcher, Louisiana. Peggy is a good cooker, and Lew is a good eater.

This is my very best neighbor, Dot. She cooks desserts, but also, too, she does a lot of cutting up.

PEGGY'S BENNE SEED BRITTLE

4 cups sesame (benne) seeds
4 cups sugar
1 cup Pet milk

Pinch salt
1 TBS. of white Karo syrup
¼ lb. margarine

Parch sesame seeds in heavy skillet on medium heat, stirring constantly until golden brown. Set aside to cool.

Combine sugar, milk, butter, salt, and syrup in heavy saucepan, and cook to soft-ball stage (240–250 degrees). Add sesame seeds and stir until mixture holds its shape. Pour into well-greased tray, preferably one with sides. Allow to cool, and then break into serving pieces.

Peggy is the MUCH better half of Lew Woods. Dey have the Airline Motors Restaurant in LaPlace, Louisiana, where I been eating good food for 40 year.

GARDEN CAKE A LA DOT

1 large angel food cake
6 egg yolks, beaten
¾ cup sugar
¾ cup lemon juice
1½ tsp. grated lemon peel

1 pkg. gelatin, dissolved in ¼ cup
   cold water
6 egg whites, stiffly beaten
¾ cup sugar added to beaten egg
   whites

Make a custard from egg yolks, sugar, juice, and lemon peel. Cook in a double boiler, until the mixture coats the spoon. Add gelatin to hot mixture and set aside to cool. Add the mixture to the beaten egg whites. Grease a large casserole. Break angel food cake into bite-size pieces into casserole. Pour mixture over cake. Place in refrigerator for at least 1 hour. DO NOT BAKE. Eat whenever!

Dot is da very bes' neighbor in da world!

RHUBARB PIE

Pie crust (see my recipe)
3 TBS. flour
1 cup sugar
1 egg, beaten

2 cups rhubarb, cut into small
   pieces
Red food coloring (optional)
Pie crust

Peel rhubarb, and remove strings. Cut into ½-inch pieces. Sift flour and sugar together. Add egg. Beat thoroughly and add rhubarb. If you use food coloring, add it now. Line pie with pastry and pour in filling. Cover with top crust. Bake at 425 degrees for 10 minutes; reduce heat to 350 degrees and bake for 35 minutes until crust is golden brown.

Arrange pastry strips in lattice design over top instead of top crust, or omit top crust. Cool slightly and cover with whipped cream.

FIG CAKE

3 TBS. sugar
1 egg
½ cup oil
1½ cups all-purpose flour
½ tsp. soda

1 tsp. baking powder
1 pint fresh ripe figs or fig jam,
   chopped fine or mashed
1 cup chopped pecans

Beat together sugar and egg. Add oil and beat. Sift together dry ingredients and add slowly while mixing. Add nuts and figs. Pour into a greased and floured 9 x 12-inch pan. Bake at 350 degrees for 30 to 35 minutes until done.

PIE CRUST

2 cups plain flour
¾ tsp. salt

½ cup shortening or peanut oil
¼ cup ice water

Mix flour and salt. Cut in shortening well. Add ice water and blend well. Flour bread board or surface you are going to use to roll out crust. Roll thickness you desire. This crust will take about 45 minutes to 1 hour to cook in a 350-degree oven, or until brown. When making fruit pies, just watch for browning.

ROASTED PECANS

3 cups Louisiana pecan halves
½ cup melted butter
Salt

Cayenne pepper or Louisiana hot sauce

Put pecan halves on baking pan. Melt butter and put hot sauce or cayenne pepper in butter. Pour butter over pecans and shake to cover. Roast nuts at 350 degrees for about 30 minutes. Be sure to shake the pan once or twice while roasting and don't burn them. Remove from oven and sprinkle with salt and more cayenne pepper if you want.

Cool and store in airtight container. You can make these ahead during pecan season and freeze until needed.

YEOLA'S BREAD PUDDING

10 slices stale bread
3 eggs, beaten
2 cups sugar
½ cup oleo
1 cup raisins
1 cup pecan pieces

1 16-ounce can fruit cocktail with juice
1 12-ounce can Pet milk
1 cup water
2 TBS. vanilla butter nut flavoring

Put everything in a large bowl and mix it up. Yeola says that she uses her hands to make sure it's well blended. Then turn into a greased 9 x 13-inch pan and bake in a 400-degree oven for 1 hour and 20 minutes.

INDEX

Andouille
  in Comforting Barbecue Sauce, 21
  Gizzard Gumbo with, 55
  Gumbo, Chicken and, 59
  Gumbo, Oyster, 56
  Sauce Piquant, Wild Duck and, 112
APPETIZERS, 17-27
Artichoke
  Boiled Burr, 139
  Salad, 33
  Soup, Oyster, 57
Au Justin Gravy, 99
Avocado
  Mos' Nilly Guacamole, 36
  Salad, Tuna and, 40

Bacon
  Embrochette Oysters and, 79
Barbecue Sauce
  Andouille in Comforting, 45
  au Justin, 48
  Comforting, 51
  Dehydrator, 45
Barbecued
  Beef Steaks on Barbecue Pit, 100
  Goat, 96
  Oysters, 79
  Pork Ribs, Smoked, 104
  Rabbit, 116
  Red Beans, 131
  Shrimp, 84
Beans
  Barbecued Red, 131
  Butter, with Ham Shanks, 141
  Red Bean Casserole, 141
Beef
  and Shrimp, Embrochette, 97
  Corned Beef Hash, Baked, 104
  Marinade and Basting Sauce for Brisket
    of, 47
  Smoked Roast, 99

Steaks on Barbecue Pit, 101
Stuffed Roast, 99
Tongue, Pickled, 105
Vegetable Soup, 60
Beer Marinade for Beef, 47
Bell Pepper, Fish-Stuffed, 83
Benne Seed Brittle, Peggy's, 151
Boston Butt and Cabbage, 97
BOUCHERIE, 117-125
Boudin
  Crawfish, 81
  Rouge, 125
  White Pork, 123
Bread Pudding, 155
BREADS, 61-68
Buttermilk Bread, 67

Cabbage
  and Onions with Louisiana Smoked
    Sausage, 129
  and Turnips, 129
  Boston Butt and, 97
  Cole Slaw, 36
  Hot Slaw with Tasso, 131
  New Year's Cabbage Rolls, 128
Cake
  Fig, 152
  Garden, a la Dot, 151
Canteloupe Sherbet, 148
Catfish
  and Crawfish Mold, 41
  Deep-Fried, 87
Cheese
  Green Salad with Romano, 40
  Hogshead, 121
  Roquefort Dressing, 39
  Tasso Pizza, 25
  Tasso Toast, 68
Chicken
  and Andouille Gumbo, 59
  Deep-Fried, 97

Gizzards and Oysters in Wine, 23
I-Wonder-What, 97
Mustard, 108
Sauce Piquant, 101
Cole Slaw, 36
Corn
    Boiled, 132
    Bread, Hot Water, 64
    Crawfish Maque-Chou, 89
    Flour Bread, 64
    in Foil, 136
    Soup, Shrimp and, 55
Couche-Couche, 68
Courtbouillion, 56
Crab
    and Crawfish Etouffée, 73
    Boiled Crabs, 85
    Crab Meat Alma, 19
    Crabby Mushrooms, 24
    Deep-Fried Soft-Shelled, 88
    How to Crack a, 75
    Stuffed, 80
Cracklin's, 121
Crawfish
    and Egg Salad, 37
    Boiled, 83
    Boudin, 81
    Etouffée, Crab and, 73
    How to Peel a, 71
    Jambalaya, 77
    Maque Chou, 89
    Mold, Catfish and, 41
    Pie, 91
    Squash and, 73
    Tails, Fried, 85
Cucumber and Onion Salad, 33

DESSERTS, 145-155
Devilish Eggs, 19
Dove Bosom, Deep-Fried, 114
Dressing, Rice and Oyster, 72
Duck
    and Andouille Sauce Piquant, Wild, 112
    with Apples, Roast, 113

Egg
    Devilish, 19
    Salad, Crawfish and, 37
    Tasso Omelet, 107

Embrochette
    Beef and Shrimp, 97
    Oyster and Bacon, 79
Etouffée
    Crab and Crawfish, 73
    Frogleg, 76

Falernum
    Chicken I-Wonder-What, 97
    Melon Balls in, 147
    Strawberry Sherbet, 147
Fig Bread, 65
Fig Cake, 152
Filé, 57
Fish
    Courtbouillion au Justin, 56
    Filets, Marinated Fried, 89
    in Tomato Sauce on Barbecue Pit, 81
    Justin's Tuna Salad, 39
    Marinade, 51
    Stuffed Bell Peppers, 83
Frogleg Etouffée, 76

GAME, 109-116
Green pepper, see Bell pepper
Grillades, 124
Grilled Potatoes, 136
Guacamole, Mos' Nilly, 35
GUMBOS AND SOUPS, 53-60

Ham, Louisiana Smoked, 101
Hogshead Cheese, 121
Hot Water Corn Bread, 64
Hush Puppies, 63

Italian Sausage in Tomato Sauce, 23
Italian Sausage Spaghetti Sauce, 108

Jambalaya, Shrimp or Crawfish, 77

Lamb Chops Broiled with Mushrooms, 103
Liver in Mustard Sauce, 95

Marinade
    All-Purpose, 49
    Beer, 47
    Fish, 51
    and Basting Sauce for Brisket of Beef, 47
MEATS, 93-108

Mirliton
    Salad with Roquefort Dressing, 39
    Smothered, 143
Mushrooms
    Crabby, 24
    Broiled Lamb Chops with, 103
Mustard Chicken, 108
Mustard Greens with Louisiana Smoked
    Sausage, 135
Mustard Sauce, Liver in, 95

Okra, Deep-Fried, 135
Omelet, Tasso, 107
Onions
    and Cucumber Salad, 36
    Baked Stuffed, with Pork, 143
    Cabbage and, with Louisiana Smoked
        Sausage, 129
Oysters
    and Andouille Gumbo, 56
    Artichoke Soup, 57
    au Justin, 76
    Barbecued, 80
    Chicken Gizzards and, in Wine, 23
    Deep-Fried, 87
    Dressing and Rice, 72
    Ed, 24
    Embrochette with Bacon, 79
    on Half Shell, Louisiana, 79
    Rockefella Casserole, 92

Pasta and Louisiana Smoked Sausage, 105
Peanuts, Boiled, 27
Pecans
    Brittle, 149
    Doris's Pralines, 149
    Roasted, 153
Peggy's Benne Seed Brittle, 151
Pepper Vinegar, 52
Pickled
    Beef Tongue, 105
    Eggs, 21
    Pork, 120
    Shrimp #1, 20
    Shrimp #2, 20
Picnic Potato Salad, 35
Pie
    Crawfish, 91
    Crust, 153

Rhubarb, 152
Pig in Cajun Microwave, 123
Pork
    Baked Stuffed Onions with Fresh, 143
    Boston Butt and Cabbage, 97
    Boudin, 123
    Pate, 124
    Pickled, 120
    Ribs, 108
    Roast, 100
    Salt, 120
    Sausage, 125
Potatoes
    Stuffed, au Wayne, 139
    Grilled, 136
    Salad, Picnic, 35
Pralines, Doris's, 149

Rabbit
    Barbecue, 116
    Stew, 116
Remoulade Sauce, 44
Rhubarb Pie, 152
Rice, 136
    and Oyster Dressing, 72
Roquefort Dressing, 40

SALADS, 29-41
Salt Pork, 120
Sauce Piquant
    Chicken, 101
    Turtle, 111
    Wild Duck and Andouille, 112
SAUCES, 43-52
Sausage
    Cabbage and Onions with Louisiana
        Smoked, 129
    Fresh Pork, 125
    in Tomato Sauce, Italian, 23
    Louisiana Smoked, 103
    Mustard Greens with Louisiana Smoked,
        135
    Pasta and Louisiana Smoked, 105
    Spaghetti Sauce, Italian, 108
    Venison, 113
SEAFOOD, 69-92
Sesame Seed Brittle, *see* Benne Seed Brittle,
    Peggy's
Sherbet
    Canteloupe, 148

Strawberry, 147
Watermelon, 147
Shortcake, Mama's Strawberry, 148
Shrimp
    Barbecue, 84
    Boiled, 88
    with Caper Sauce, 84
    and Corn Soup, 55
    Pickled, 20
    Salad, 32
    Soup, 59
Smoked Barbecued Pork Ribs, 104
Smoked Beef Roast and Pork Roast, 99
Smoked Pickled Eggs, 21
Smothered Mirliton, 143
Spaghetti, 133
Spaghetti Sauce, Italian Sausage, 108
Squash
    and Crawfish, 73
    Deep-Fried, 132
    Maurice, 137
Stew
    Rabbit, 116
    Turtle, 114
Strawberry
    Sherbet, 147
    Shortcake, Mama's, 148
Stuffed Beef and Pork Roasts, 100
Sweet Potatoes
    Baked, 137
    Bread, 65

Tartar Sauce, 44
Tasso, 25
    Hot Slaw with, 131
    Omelet, 107
    Toast, 68
Tomato
    and Onion Salad, 36
    Sauce, Fish in, 81
    Sauce, Italian Sausage with, 23
Tongue
    Baked, 96
    Pickled, 105
Tuna
    and Avocado Salad, 40
    Salad, Justin's, 39
Turkey, Deep-Fried, 95
Turnips, Cabbage and, 129
Turtle
    Sauce Piquant, 111
    Stew, 114

Vegetable Soup, 60
VEGETABLES, 127-143
Venison Sausage, 113

Watermelon Sherbet, 147